MANAGEMENT PLANNING AND CONTROL IN INFLATION

By the same author

MANAGEMENT CONTROL AND INFORMATION
(*with R. Beresford Dew*)

MANAGEMENT PLANNING AND CONTROL IN INFLATION

Kenneth P. Gee

Senior Lecturer
Department of Accounting and Finance
University of Lancaster

First published 1977 by
THE MACMILLAN PRESS LTD
London and Basingstoke
Associated companies in Delhi
Dublin Hong Kong Johannesburg Lagos
Melbourne New York Singapore Tokyo

British Library Cataloguing in Publication Data

Gee, Kenneth Philip
  Management planning and control in inflation
  1. Industrial management and inflation
  2. Corporations — Finance
  I. Title
  658.1'5   HG4028.I/

ISBN 0–333–22070–6

Printed in Great Britain by
Billing & Sons Limited
Guildford, London and Worcester

This book is sold subject
to the standard conditions
of the Net Book Agreement

Contents

Preface   vii

1 NATURE AND SCOPE OF THIS BOOK   1
  1.1 Introduction   1
  1.2 Two recurrent themes   2
  1.3 Limitations and disclaimers   4

2 THE PROCESS OF CAPITAL PROJECT PLANNING   6
  2.1 The impact of indexed finance   6
  2.2 The uses of equity and indexed debt   10
  2.3 An example of an investment proposal   12
  2.4 Division of labour in project appraisal   14
  2.5 Modelling on a current accruals basis   16
  2.6 Modelling operating and capital flows   22
  2.7 Cash flows from debt financing   24
  2.8 Cash flows from taxes and grants   26
  2.9 Constructing the net terminal value   28
  2.10 The process of evaluation   31
  2.11 A link between planning and control   35

3 THE PROCESS OF DIVISIONAL CONTROL   37
  3.1 Recommendations in outline   37
  3.2 Direct materials costs under Sandilands   39
  3.3 Fixed assets—controllability of costs and gains   42
  3.4 The treatment of inventory   46
  3.5 Charging for invested working capital: 48
    (a) Determining the rate of charge   48
    (b) Measuring the capital base   52
    (c) The accrual—cash flow distinction   55
    (d) The effect on an investment proposal   56
  3.6 Assessing managerial and economic performance   58
  3.7 Signalling disposal investigations   61
  3.8 Signalling expansion investigations   62
  3.9 Performance measures: summarisation and interaction   63
  3.10 Broader comparisons and wider problems   65
  Appendix: The argument against return on capital   67

4 THE INTEGRATED PLANNING-CONTROL
PROCESS: PURCHASING   70
  4.1 Motives for inventory acquisiton   70
  4.2 Inflation in the simplest EOQ model   71
  4.3 Performance implications of purchasing decisions   73
  4.4 Dysfunctional consequences of current cost measurement 76
  4.5 Comparison against an optimal budget: Forecasting errors 77
  4.6 Comparison against an optimal budget: Adaptation errors 83
  4.7 Forecasting and adaptation errors: Inventory flow problems 86
  4.8 Some limitations of this analysis   91

5 A FURTHER OUTLOOK   94
  5.1 Inflation and management: Stimulus and response   94
  5.2 Three small extensions of the analysis: 95
    (a) Short-term cash budgeting   95
    (b) Divisional financial performance in context 97
    (c) Evaluating purchasing decisions by reference to the time value of money 98
  5.3 The permanence of inflationary problems for management 101

Notes to Chapters 1–5   103

Glossary of algebraic symbols used   111

Bibliography   114

Author index   119

Subject index   121

Preface

The Sandilands Report [83]* and the IASG response to it [52] have between them opened up the possibility of using in accounting a wide variety of valuation concepts. In a critical review of Sandilands, Chambers [25, pp. 34–6] has pointed out that it will involve the accountant in using no less than five valuation concepts; historic cost, net realisable value, replacement cost, present value and (for monetary items) face value. To these five distinct concepts, the IASG [52, ch. 19] seem now to have added a sixth concept of price-level adjusted historic cost (PLAHC). Some authors, like Chambers, may bemoan the employment of this variety of approaches to accounting valuation, and fear that the end-result may simply be confusion. It is the endeavour of this book to try to sort out some of the potential sources of confusion for the management accountant inherent in the move to Current Cost Accounting. At different stages of the book, five of the six accounting valuation concepts referred to above will be placed in their context and shown to have a part to play in improving the process of management planning and control.

The odd man out among the six valuation concepts turns out to be PLAHC. A recent U.S. study by Shank [88] has indicated that managers do not perceive price-level adjusted financial statements to be useful, even where they fully understand their content. Providing managers with price-level adjusted as well as historic cost financial statements for an enterprise did not cause them to change their opinions concerning that enterprise's financial policy, even though the price-level adjusted statements showed a very different picture to that portrayed by the historic cost statements.

Having said this, general price level adjustments might still enter the process of managerial decision-making if they were to be used as a basis for the determination of taxable income. This author believes, with Morley [73, p. 108], that it would be impossible to place corporate taxation on a current cost accounting basis since this would lack the

* Reference numbers in square brackets refer to publications listed in the bibliography at the end of this book. Similarly, superior numbers in the text relate to the notes at the back of the book.

necessary objectivity (as well as raising severe difficulties for small firms who had not the resources to install the relatively sophisticated accounting systems that would be required). Consequently, if corporate taxation were to be thoroughly adjusted for inflation, it would be necessary to base taxation upon general price-level accounting. As a result, price-level adjusted historic costs would require to be forecast as inputs to the tax side of capital budgeting decisions such as those examined in Chapter 2. Until and unless this major tax reform is undertaken, however, PLAHC must remain the 'Cinderella' among valuation concepts insofar as management accounting is concerned.

But all of the remaining five accounting valuation concepts play more or less active parts in the analysis of this book, with replacement cost in a pivotal role. In fact, one way of looking at this book would be to say that it explores the cliché that different accounting valuation concepts may be appropriate for different purposes, by indicating which valuation concepts may best serve certain *specific* purposes within management accounting.

These specific purposes have been chosen fairly narrowly, and this book makes no claim whatever to be a general survey of management accounting under inflationary conditions. It consists in essence of three substantial sections. The first uses terminal value (a variant of present value) to examine capital budgeting under conditions of inflation and indexation. Following from this, the second section uses all five accounting valuation concepts in an examination of divisional performance measurement, which leads into the third section's study of an aspect of performance measurement within the division, namely the measurement of purchasing performance. An introductory chapter outlines the plan of the book, its context and the relationship between the sections, while the final chapter advances three extensions of the analysis and indicates why there is a need for further study.

I owe an enormous debt of gratitude to a remarkably large number of people for their help during the preparation of this book. I must start by thanking my colleagues, initially at UMIST and later at the University of Lancaster; both places provided constant intellectual stimulus as well as practical support. In the latter context special mention must be made of Mrs Pam Breslin, who typed the many drafts through which this book went. My thanks go to those who sat through presentations of the drafts at conferences of the British Accounting and Finance Association and the Association of University Teachers of Accounting; my most profound thanks go to those who were sufficiently stirred by the presentations to comment critically. This book, incidentally, supersedes all those conference papers and indeed all my published and un-published work from 1974–76 with the exception of Gee and Peasnell [38].

My final thanks must go to two people. First, to Mrs M. Sedgwick, who typed the final text of this book so well. Second (yet most fundamentally of all) my heartfelt thanks must go to my wife, Hilary; I am quite certain that without her constant encouragement and support this book would never have been written. It is dedicated to her.

Kenneth P. Gee

December 1976

1 Nature and Scope of this Book

1.1 Introduction

Inflation is not a new phenomenon, but the 1970s have seen a marked and sustained acceleration of inflation throughout the countries of the industrialised West. Recently, Dale [28] has reported an OECD forecast suggesting inflation rates of at least 7–8 % p.a. for these countries over the period 1975–80. The forecast rates vary from country to country, that for the U.K. being 10–12 % p.a. Over the longer term, an extremely sophisticated simulation for the U.S. economy by Ibbotson and Sinquefield [50] gave a mean inflation rate of just over 6 % p.a. for the period 1976–2000; a conclusion which they qualified by asserting that there was a 5 % probability that inflation would exceed 11.3 % p.a. over that period and a 5 % probability that it would be less than 2 % p.a. Inflation estimates are clearly subject to a high degree of uncertainty – and a particular 'inflation rate' for a country represents no more than a weighted average of a large number of individual price movements. Within an inflationary economy, the inflation rates appropriate to particular commodities vary widely; some prices may double in a year while others remain almost constant. It would seem plain that the complex interaction of large absolute and relative price changes must have enormous implications for management decision-making.

Yet these implications have seldom been brought together and spelled out. Despite the considerable importance of this topic, despite the imminence of the change in the basic measuring-rod of accounting from historic cost to current cost, the subject of management accounting under inflation has suffered a remarkable neglect. A great deal has been written about inflation accounting, to be sure, but it has been mainly concerned with *reporting* the implications of past transactions to *outsiders*. The equally important task of *analysing* the implications of past and future transactions for the benefit of *internal* management has received surprisingly little attention.

This book, then, is concerned with the impact of price changes on the process of managerial planning and control in divisionalised enterprises. In the next chapter attention is concentrated upon capital budgeting decisions and the long-term planning process, while in the following chapter the focus switches to the financial control process at divisional level. Finally, an integrated planning-control process within the division is analysed, and a concluding chapter provides a further outlook upon the broad problems of the book.

In moving from planning to control, this book follows the cycle of managerial activity, and in attempting to integrate planning and control it recognises that such activity *is* cyclical – so that no part of the cycle can be considered in isolation. To be more explicit, the book takes as its framework the diagrammatic illustration shown below of the functions of management.

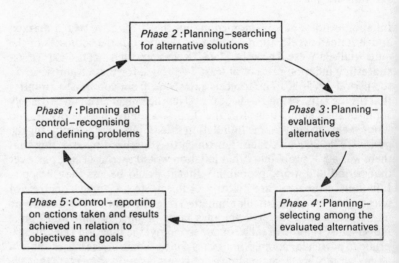

This representation of the planning and control function as an endless loop is derived from ASOBAT [3, p. 50]. In its terms this book enters the loop at Phase 3 and follows it round to Phase 1, omitting only Phase 2 from consideration. Of course, each phase is not considered in its entirety – attention is confined in Phases 3 and 4 to capital budgeting, in Phase 5 to divisional performance measurement and in Phase 1 to certain aspects of purchasing. The intention is to sample each phase not to provide a comprehensive study of the impact of inflation upon each one. With the present state of knowledge, it would be presumptuous to attempt more.

1.2 Two recurrent themes

At this stage, two themes must be introduced which will recur throughout the book. The first of these is divisionalisation, with its accompanying requirement that the interests of each division should as far as possible be made to coincide with the interests of the company as a whole. For the purposes of this book, the term division will be restricted to separately accountable units within profit-seeking organisations. No unit can be said to be a division unless the financial performance measures against which it is assessed involve both costs and revenues.

The practice of splitting up large companies into separate profit-responsible divisions has recently become much more widespread in Europe. As Franko [35, p. 493] points out:

Tariffs were abolished within the European Economic Community (EEC) on July 1, 1968. This date marked an acceleration of changes in the structures of large European organizations. After half a century of structural stability, 38 of the 81 large Swiss, Italian, German, French, Dutch, Swedish and Belgian companies on the Fortune list of the 200 largest non-American industrials announced major changes in structure by the end of 1972.

These changes, Franko says, 'almost invariably involved shifts toward the more American multidivisional structure,' (p. 494) and he also quotes Stopford's data to the effect that such changes have been at least as extensive in the United Kingdom (where they took place rather earlier).

This author believes with Williamson [100, pp. 139–41] that where the activities of a company are not overwhelmingly interdependent [1] the divisionalised structure has a number of advantages over the functional structure. But it is not within the scope of this book to argue the case for and against divisionalisation. Instead, the divisionalised structure will simply be accepted as a fact of commercial life — its very pervasiveness justifying the concentration of this book upon it. This concentration, however, will not be absolute. Much of what will be said in Chapters 2 and 4 about capital budgeting and purchasing will be applicable to non-divisionalised organisations; only Chapter 3 on performance measurement will be totally confined in its applicability to a divisionalised context.

The second of this book's recurrent themes is not organisational but financial. It relates to the need to distinguish between profits and net cash flows in an inflationary period. The more rapidly inflation progresses, the more profit will tend to run ahead of net cash flow, and this effect may well give rise to erroneous management decisions if it is not fully understood. This danger is particularly acute for long-term decisions, which is why this book lays particular stress on the profit-net cash flow distinction when discussing capital budgeting. The distinction, however, also has an impact upon shorter-term decisions, and especially upon the appraisal of divisional performance. Hence it will recur, with a somewhat lesser emphasis, in section 3.5(c) of this book.

Recently, evidence has been advanced to the effect that U.K. managers are becoming increasingly conscious of the profit-net cash flow distinction. Tweedie has carried out two surveys of managers asking the question 'what does inflation mean to you?' – the first in 1968 and the second in 1975. He tabulates his findings in a paper [96, p. 12], showing that in 1968 none of the managers identified cash flow problems as arising from inflation, while in 1975 11 % of the sample surveyed did so. This must be read in the context of p. 6 of the same study, which indicates an increasing focus by managers on the effect of inflation upon their work rather than upon their personal circumstances or upon the state of the nation as a whole. While in 1968 only 8 % of the managers identified inflation's main impact as being upon their work, by 1975 this had risen to 55 %.

Thus there seems to be a need for studies of 'inflation and management'. Indeed, broad studies already exist, notably those by Hussey [48], West [98], Ashton and Morrell [9] and Cox and Hewgill [27]. This book is closest in spirit to the last of these, though more specific and narrowly-focused. It is concerned with the response of complex divisionalised organisations to an inflation which manifests itself not only in a rising general price level but also in increasing fluctuations of relative prices. The book asks how the planning and control process, which is stressful for large and complex enterprises under any circumstances, can be sustained at all in so turbulent a financial environment. While particular solutions must always depend on particular circumstances, it is nonetheless hoped that some general guidelines may be laid down to assist in designing planning and control systems. The derivation of such guidelines constitutes the purpose of this book.

1.3 Limitations and disclaimers

Having indicated the general scope of this book, it may be as well to round off this introduction by outlining some limitations and disclaimers. Emphasis must be placed from the start upon the extremely tentative nature of this text. It is intended here merely to provide an outline map of the new environment in which the financial planning and control of divisionalised enterprises must be carried out. In places, the assumptions employed may well be considered exceedingly restrictive, but this restrictiveness is necessary for the analysis to proceed at all. Later studies will no doubt relax or abandon many of the assumptions made here, and indeed a major function of this study may be to indicate those areas where tightly-drawn assumptions signal that further work is urgently required.

The next point may not be considered a limitation at all, but is certainly a disclaimer from the point of view of theory. A crucial consideration in the design of this book has been that the calculations within it should depend upon variables which it is feasible for management to measure and forecast. To take an important example, the 'weighted average cost of capital' concept has been rejected for this book on the grounds that whatever its merits are in principle it is far too uncertain of computation in practice. Similarly, the postaudit of capital projects has been excluded in the belief that there is normally no operational way of splitting out the cash flows associated with a particular project from those of the enterprise as a whole. When writing as an academic, it is tempting to forget responsibility to a practitioner audience. In endeavouring to avoid this temptation, this book has at least tried to confine itself to operational concepts.

As a final point, this book does not pretend to be comprehensive even in dealing with the limited range of topics which it covers. In discussing capital budgeting the complications introduced by capital rationing are not mentioned, while the study of divisional performance measurement does not deal with the problems posed by inter-divisional trading and the examination of purchasing builds only upon the simplest EOQ model. The concern throughout is to examine those parts of the above three topics which are directly affected by the existence of inflation. Other aspects which are not so directly affected have simply been left out of consideration.

Now that the scope and nature of this book has been fixed and its context and boundaries have been established, the point has been reached at which the body of the book can be entered. The reader is encouraged to follow the author step by step through the analysis which follows.

2 The Process of Capital Project Planning

2.1 The impact of indexed finance

In this chapter the reader is asked to visualise the current U.K. financial environment, then to superimpose upon it one significant change. Suppose that the Government were to institute a savings scheme to which loans of any size could be made by individuals or corporations, repayable on demand. These loans would carry no interest, but their principal would be linked to the Retail Price Index. Thus £100 lent when the Index stood at 100 would lead to a repayment of £150 if during the life of this loan the Index were to rise 50%. Returns of principal would not be subject to tax, and there would be no transactions costs. A lender of money on these terms would be vulnerable neither to unexpectedly rapid inflation[1] nor to any risk of default, and could consequently be described as holding a real risk-free asset. The issue of such a real risk-free asset in the form of gilt-edged stock seems likely in the near future, as part of a Government strategy aimed at reducing the Exchequer cash outlay on interest, which would in turn help to restrain the public sector borrowing requirement. In a sense, the idea of a real risk-free asset is not novel – all it involves is the removal of restrictions from the index-linked savings certificates and SAYE schemes which already exist.

The tax treatment of real risk-free assets is crucial, and will be taken as being the same whoever issues them. Following Brazilian practice quoted by Kafka [54, p. 92] two assumptions will be made; first that repayments of indexed principal are tax-free to their recipients and second that the indexed portion of such repayments is deductible against Corporation Tax. Thus if it were a company rather than the Government issuing the real risk-free asset in the numerical example above, the £50 represented by the excess of the principal repayment over the amount borrowed would be tax-deductible. The treatment of interest payments will be assumed to be unchanged, such payments being tax-deductible by the borrower and taxable as income or profit when received by the lender. All of the interest paid or received is to be treated in this fashion, irrespective of whether or not the interest is computed on an indexed basis.[2]

There is, of course, no U.K. experience of a real risk-free asset, so that the reaction of financial markets to it can only be conjectured. To avoid speculating in a vacuum, it will be assumed that U.K. financial markets respond in the same way to the existence of a real risk-free asset as did Brazilian markets after their government first issued an indexed security in 1964. This leaves open the question, though, of why financial markets should respond at all to this innovation. To understand the implications of introducing a real risk-free asset, it is necessary at the outset to contrast it with the traditional 'risk-free asset' represented by a fixed interest Government security held to maturity. This is risk-free only in the trivial sense of bearing no risk of default. 'Trivial' because any investor can, by holding a sufficiently diversified portfolio of fixed interest securities, render the consequences to him of a default on any one of those securities insignificant. By contrast, the inflation risk associated with holding fixed interest securities cannot be diversified away in this fashion. As Keane [55, p. 135] points out:

Included in the nominal rate of interest on loan capital is a fixed percentage representing the expected change in the value of money, and it is evident that if the future rate of inflation is subject to uncertainty, then the concept of a 'risk-free' fixed income security is untenable.

Thus the introduction of a real risk-free asset would create an investment opportunity different in kind from those already existing. The consequences of introducing such an asset may be traced from Brazilian experience as follows: For a start, there would be a major impact on the banking system. This would arise from extensive switching out of bank deposits into the real risk-free asset, which in turn would compel the banks to offer indexed deposits in order to compete. These indexed deposits must for prudence be matched against indexed advances, so that bank loans and overdrafts would in future be made on indexed terms. More precisely, such loans would have their principal indexed and would also carry an (indexed) rate of interest to compensate for their default risk. [3]

Even without indexation of government borrowing, it seems that the U.K. market for longer-term fixed interest securities may gradually be disappearing – in 1975 net issues of loan capital were only £30M as against equity issues of £955M. Cornell [26, ch. 6] has recently outlined a plausible explanation for the drying-up of this market in periods of rapid and variable inflation. His argument may best be illustrated by reference to a numerical example. Suppose a firm borrows at 17% p.a. for ten years at a time when the actual (and expected) rate of inflation is 15% p.a. There is then a change of government policy such that next year the actual (and expected) rate of inflation drops to 10% p.a. and stays at that level over the remaining nine years of the loan's life. Assuming for convenience that the real rate of interest is independent of the inflation rate, this would imply that had the firm held off borrowing for one year it could have raised a ten-year loan at 12%, not 17%. Relative to competitors who did not borrow long when the expected rate of inflation was 15%, this firm will have high financing costs over the next nine years. But on the other hand if the change of government policy were instead to raise the actual (and expected) rate of inflation to 20% p.a. then those who had lent to the firm at 17% p.a. would have missed the opportunity (given a constant real rate of interest) to make a ten-year loan at 22% p.a. after the policy change. Relative to other investors who refrained from lending long when the expected inflation rate was 15%, these investors would have poor interest receipts over the remaining nine years of their loan's life. Thus inflation risk can work against the interests of either borrowers or lenders, and both can minimise their exposure to this risk by avoiding long-term financial transactions. As increasing uncertainty about future inflation rates gives both borrowers and lenders an increasingly strong motive to preserve their freedom to recontract, the market for long-term fixed interest securities correspondingly dries up.

Clearly, the existence of transactions costs and of differing inflationary expectations on the parts of borrowers and lenders will impose limits upon this process of shortening debt duration. But a strong trend in the direction of shorter debt has been observed in Canada and the U.S.A. (as well as the U.K.) during periods of considerable inflation rate uncertainty. The introduction of a real risk-free asset is likely to accelerate the decline of the long-term fixed interest market, in that such an asset provides certainty of real interest costs and revenues to borrowers and lenders. This contrasts with the very great uncertainty of real interest costs and revenues shown in the numerical example above. The avoidance of such uncertainty benefits both borrowers and lenders – which may go a long way toward explaining why economies with extensive indexation (such as Brazil and Israel) have not had a substantial long-term fixed interest market coexisting with the market for indexed finance.

Examination of the Brazilian market for indexed finance yields a curious finding. The above argument would suggest that as more experience was obtained of indexation, long-term indexed loans would become progressively more popular. Yet after more than ten years of such experience, a market for long-term indexed loans has simply failed to emerge in Brazil. Huyck [49, p. 61] indicates that the investment banks set up there in 1966 were conceived as supplying loans of this nature to the private sector for fixed capital investment. However, in 1975 Branford [17] pointed out:

Apart from repass operations with government funds, the investment banks supply about 30 times more resources for working capital and short-term loans than for investment purposes, which alone shows that they are not fulfilling the function for which they were created.

The absence of a market for indexed long-term finance of any kind is confirmed by Bhatia [14, p. 33], Kafka [54, p. 91] and McMahon [70, p. 78]. A major part of the reason for it may be found in the Brazilian system of price control. This is described by DeVoe [30, p. 41] in the following terms:

Firms are allowed to raise prices to the extent of approved increases in wage rates and other costs, less an arbitrarily determined standard productivity improvement. Of course some firms cannot achieve the standard productivity improvement, and their margins can contract substantially or disappear. Businesses that violate or exceed the permitted price levels can be deprived of access to credit from the banking system.

Much of this has a familiar ring to U.K. ears. The implication of continuing price controls of this nature must be to render at least some forms of long-term indexed debt extremely hazardous to the borrower. In a modern U.K. context, a prudent management must bear in mind the possibility that price controls which do not allow the passing-on of unavoidable cost increases will be imposed unilaterally and without warning. These controls are likely to depress the rate of growth of corporate profits below the currently-prevailing rate of increase of the Retail Price Index (RPI). A firm which has issued debt linked to this index will then find that debt servicing costs come to absorb an increasing proportion of profits.[4] Where price controls are persistent, a firm which has incurred long-term RPI-linked debt will find itself facing a more sustained and severe liquidity crisis than will a firm that can rearrange its financial position as its short-term indexed debt is redeemed. It does not seem unreasonable to suggest that the fear of financial inflexibility in the face of price controls may act as a deterrent to the issue of long-term indexed debt in the U.K., as it seems to have done in Brazil.

This fear, however, will not necessarily inhibit the incurrence of *short-term* indexed indebtedness. Vulnerability to price control effects will in any case be much reduced if the index to which debt is linked is specific to the borrower's industry rather than economy-wide. In practice, firms undertaking indexed debt have tended to link it to a price index relating to the commodity which they produce. An Israeli example of this is represented by the Nesher Cement Company's 1952 issue of bonds linked to the official price of cement, while in France the 1953 railway issue was linked to the level of rail fares. The advantage of this approach is that the amount paid out in interest and principal will rise only when industry prices increase. To the extent that price increases tend to be associated with higher profitability and therefore greater debt servicing capacity, this type of financing contains a built-in safety factor. It is also true, conversely, that if price control legislation has a disproportionately severe effect on a particular industry's prices, then firms within that industry using this method of indexed financing will find their debt servicing costs correspondingly restrained.

In the context of this argument, it will be supposed that banks competing with the real risk-free asset insist that their advances must be linked to the Wholesale Price Index (WPI) relating to the borrower's product. Major banks with an economy-wide spread of lending would then have a loan portfolio which was in aggregate linked to the level of wholesale prices in the economy. This would enable such banks to link their deposits to the Retail Price Index (and therefore compete directly with the real risk-free asset) in the knowledge that changes in wholesale price indices would change their receipts from loans to compensate for subsequent changes in payments to depositors as WPI changes fed through to the RPI.

To summarise this chapter so far, it may be conjectured from Brazilian experience that the impact of indexed finance in the form of a real risk-free asset would be felt in three directions:

(i) the indexation of bank deposits (and therefore advances) to avoid a drain of funds in the direction of the real risk-free asset

(ii) the acceleration of the existing decline in the market for long-term fixed interest finance

(iii) the general withdrawal of long-term finance other than through equities, arising from the difficulty that such finance would encounter in competing with a real risk-free asset repayable on demand. This difficulty would be especially acute where price control legislation was applied on a sustained basis.

The outcome of all this would be to leave equity and short-term indexed debt as the two major sources of funds, a situation which McMahon [70, p. 78] implies is to be found in contemporary Brazil. It is the purpose of this chapter to analyse a capital budgeting decision which is to be taken under conditions of inflation and with these two sources of funds. Particular attention is to be paid to the role of working capital, and many of the comments made in that context will be applicable to financing regimes other than the one directly under study here. The author therefore hopes that even those who cannot accept wholeheartedly a prophecy of 'Brazilianisation' of U.K. company finance may nonetheless find something of value in this study.

2.2 The uses of equity and indexed debt

Given that the two available sources of finance are equity and short-term indexed debt, the question which immediately arises is one of defining the most appropriate use for each source. As a preliminary to studying this, it is necessary to be rather more explicit about the nature of the short-term indexed debt. What is being contemplated here is an arrangement of an overdraft nature, carrying an (indexed) interest rate of 6% p.a. and with both interest and principal linked to a specified wholesale price index.[5] The mechanics of this arrangement are best illustrated by considering a year in which there are no new borrowings or repayments. At the beginning of the year £100 is owed, and during its course the wholesale price index concerned moves up 15%. The principal owed at the end of this year would then be £115, and the interest payments[6] would amount to $(0.06) (1.15)^{0.5} (£100) = £6.43$. It will be recalled that the real risk-free asset offers no interest; the purpose of interest here is to compensate for the default risk of the loan.

At this stage, the unusual step will be taken of associating specific financing sources with particular types of asset to be financed. (For a critique of the alternative 'weighted average cost of capital' approach, see section 3.5(a) below). In precise terms, it will be assumed that investments in working capital (represented by inventories plus debtors minus creditors) are financed by short-term indexed debt while investments in fixed assets are financed by equity. As Jones [53] has recently pointed out, such an assumption could lead to very unsatisfactory results in a financing regime without indexation – but where there is indexation it may be far more defensible. The defence for it would run as follows:

In order to compete with the real risk-free asset, commercial indexed debt must at least notionally be repayable on demand. Even if this is not interpreted literally, the implication remains that this debt should be self-liquidating, i.e. repayable within the period of a single working capital cycle. So long as indexed debt is confined to the financing of working capital assets, this self-liquidating requirement presents no problem. As debt servicing cost rises with the wholesale price index, then so (presumably) does the net realisable value (NRV) of the product at the end of the working capital cycle.[7] Investments in fixed assets, however, are not of this self-liquidating nature. If £100K is invested in a fixed asset at the beginning of a year during which the relevant wholesale price index rises 20%, it cannot be presumed that the operating cash flows from the asset during the year together with its end-year NRV will be sufficient to meet a demand for the repayment of £120K principal and (at 6% p.a.) £6573 of indexed interest. Fixed assets are thus seen to be inherently unsuitable for financing through indexed debt. They are consequently left to be financed through equity, which in an indexed regime fulfils a genuinely risk-bearing role and obtains as a reward a share in real profit growth.

The idea of linking working capital with indexed debt and fixed assets with equity lies less in the realms of fantasy than might be supposed. A recent example of finance organised on precisely this basis was provided by the British Steel Corporation. As 'Lex' [63] reported, they proposed to negotiate three-year indexed loans from the institutions, to be used to finance steel inventories. Interest on these loans was to have been linked to the Retail Price Index, while repayments of principal were to have been linked to steel prices. Though the proposal was thwarted for political reasons it may well provide an indicator of future trends.

A situation has now been postulated in which there are two major sources of finance, and the uses to which each of them may be put have been explored. The purpose of this chapter is to outline an approach to investment appraisal under these financial conditions. To keep the discussion from becoming unduly abstract, a numerical example of a fairly familiar kind will be employed. The basic facts relating to it are outlined in the next section.

2.3 An example of an investment proposal

For the purposes of the subsequent discussion, it will be necessary to specify a particular organisational context. Consider, therefore, Company R, which at the beginning of January 1979 finds itself operating in the financial environment which has been described above. Company R is a divisionalised enterprise, and one of its segments, Division Q, has just generated a capital investment proposal. This will involve the acquisition of plant and machinery to be installed in existing premises for the production of a mechanical engineering product called a vader. It will take two years to set up the machinery, so that vader production is expected to commence in January 1981. Vaders are high-technology items with a fairly short life-cycle, and experience in the industry suggests that they will be wholly obsolete by the end of 1986. The plant and machinery will then be sold in a market so thin that little more than scrap value can be expected.

Before proceeding to discuss the costs and revenues associated with the vader project, a fundamental distinction must be made. It is of vital importance to distinguish base prices and costs from current prices and costs, where these terms are defined as follows:

Base prices and costs are those prices and costs prevailing upon the 'base date' at which a capital budgeting decision is to be taken. Here the 'base date' is January 1979.

Current prices and costs are those prices and costs which, it is forecast, will currently be prevailing at a date to be specified. Thus 'current prices for 1982' sometimes abbreviated to '1982 prices' are those prices which are forecast to prevail during the course of 1982.

The first step in exploring the financial implications of the vader project involves a computation of its forecast pre-tax costs and revenues expressed in terms of January 1979 prices. What follows is this computation carried out in chronological order, starting with the initial capital costs and going through the operating costs and revenues to finish with the scrap receipts.

Dealing first then with capital costs, define a variable as follows:

K_j is the capital expenditure at base prices to be undertaken in year j (and is obtained by valuing the items to be purchased in year j at January 1979 prices.)

Assigning $j = 1$ to 1979, $j = 2$ to 1980 and so on, the following figures are derived: [8]

$$K_1 = 57, \ K_2 = 133, \ K_3 \text{ et seq.} = 0$$

Moving on to operating revenues and costs, define:

S_j is the forecast base-price sales revenue for year j. It is calculated by multiplying the quantities of vaders that are forecast to be sold in year j by the £20 per vader market price prevailing in January 1979. This gives rise to the following figures (in thousands of pounds).

$$S_1 = 0 \quad S_3 = 125 \quad S_5 = 360 \quad S_7 = 285$$
$$S_2 = 0 \quad S_4 = 285 \quad S_6 = 360 \quad S_8 = 135$$

The operating costs may be split up into materials, labour and (all other) expenses. Dealing with the last two first, define:

L_j is the forecast base-cost of labour in year j, obtained by multiplying the amounts of labour forecast to be used in year j by the wage rates prevailing in January 1979. This calculation yields:

$$L_1 = 0 \quad L_3 = 39 \quad L_5 = 72 \quad L_7 = 57$$
$$L_2 = 0 \quad L_4 = 57 \quad L_6 = 72 \quad L_8 = 27$$

E_j is the forecast base-cost of expenses in year j, obtained by multiplying the physical volume of expense items forecast to be used in year j by their cost per unit as in January 1979. The figures here are shown below:

$$E_1 = 0 \quad E_3 = 40 \quad E_5 = 62 \quad E_7 = 51$$
$$E_2 = 0 \quad E_4 = 51 \quad E_6 = 62 \quad E_8 = 38$$

A difficulty arises with materials, since unlike labour and expenses they can be stored from one year to another. The approach taken is therefore to work from the materials used through the inventory position to derive the materials purchased, as follows:

M_{uj} is the forecast base-cost of materials used in year j, obtained by multiplying the amount of materials forecast to be used in year j by the unit cost of materials prevailing in January 1979. This gives:

$$M_{u1} = 0 \quad M_{u3} = 37 \quad M_{u5} = 82 \quad M_{u7} = 65$$
$$M_{u2} = 0 \quad M_{u4} = 65 \quad M_{u6} = 82 \quad M_{u8} = 35$$

R_j is the forecast stock (at base-cost) of materials to be held at the beginning of year j. It is derived by multiplying the amounts of materials forecast to be held at the beginning of year j by the unit costs of materials prevailing in January 1979. Division Q's management, in assessing the vader project, have assumed that at the beginning of each year of its life there will be three months' requirements of materials in stock, so that $M_{uj} = 4R_j$. Using this relationship, together with the forecasts of M_{uj} above, it is possible to work out the value of materials bought (at base-cost) in year j. If this is given by M_{bj}, then:

$$M_{bj} = R_{j+1} + M_{uj} - R_j \qquad (2-1)$$

Performing the required arithmetic gives rise to the following results:

$$M_{b1} = 0 \quad M_{b3} = 44 \quad M_{b5} = 82 \quad M_{b7} = 58$$
$$M_{b2} = 9 \quad M_{b4} = 69 \quad M_{b6} = 78 \quad M_{b8} = 26$$

Having been through the capital and operating costs, it remains only to deal with the scrap receipts arising at the end of the vader project's life:

H_j is the estimated net realisable value (at base-prices) of the plant and machinery when it is sold at the end of year j. Here, the project is to terminate at the end of 1986, at which time it is estimated that the plant will realise only one-tenth of its original cost, giving it a net realisable value of $H_8 = 19$.

2.4 Division of labour in project appraisal

The management of Division Q have at this stage developed estimates of the capital costs, sales, operating costs and scrap receipts for the vader project. All of these estimates have been couched in terms of base-prices and base-costs. They represent necessary inputs to the decision as to whether to undertake the vader project, but are by themselves a quite insufficient basis on which to take that decision. A great deal more work remains to be done on the project proposal, and the nature of this work makes it better suited to the financial analysis staff at the headquarters of Company R. It is therefore proposed that Division Q should submit the financial information given so far (and no more) to Company R headquarters. The task of the HQ staff will be to convert these pre-tax, base-date costs and revenues into after-tax net cash flows expressed in terms of current prices and costs, i.e. those forecast to prevail in the years concerned. There are two reasons why this task of conversion is better performed centrally than in the divisions:

(i) Performing project appraisal centrally enables common assumptions to be applied to a range of projects. It is, for example, extremely important that the same rates of inflation should be applied to the same items of cost and revenue as between one project and another. Unless this is done, the comparison of alternatives will be rendered meaningless. Similarly, consistent assumptions about forecast tax rates, credit policy, financing arrangements and so on should be applied throughout in arriving at the capital budget. It is much easier to ensure consistency in the application of assumptions if the same impartial staff managers work on the financial appraisal of competing projects.

(ii) Expanding upon the point of impartiality, if divisional managers are left free to make such forecasts about inflation, tax and other exogenous variables as they think appropriate, there is a great danger that they may 'juggle' the values of these variables until projects to which they are personally committed attain the required level of return. As Ijiri [51, p. 27] points out:

Management's reluctance to accept an output from a complicated mathematical model may be attributed at least in part to the . . . human factor. If one attempts to justify a decision by means of a mathematical model, a complicated model with many parameters is preferable because a decision can more easily be proved to be optimum since a greater number of parameters can be manipulated within their reasonable ranges. In fact, if a model is sufficiently complicated, it is likely that any decision can be shown to be optimum by a proper choice of parameter values that are not unreasonable.

Capital investment appraisal by its very nature must involve a large number of parameter values. Consequently, a balance needs to be struck between letting divisional management make so many unverifiable estimates that project proposals become mere assertions of divisional solidarity,[9] and confining divisional management to estimating so few parameter values that important inputs from their 'local' knowledge are suppressed.

The division of labour proposed here is more vulnerable to the latter defect than the former, since it involves Company R's central staff in applying a fairly complex process of conversion to the rather basic project data supplied by Division Q (as shown above). The process of conversion starts with modelling on an accruals basis, and it is to this that attention is now turned.

2.5 Modelling on a current accruals basis

This stage of the process is concerned to compute two sets of numbers, representing:

(i) the taxable profits from operations, i.e. taxable profits prior to the deduction of interest, capital allowances and the (tax-deductible) premium on the redemption of indexed debt [10]

(ii) the capital costs upon which tax allowances and development grants are to be based.

These sets of numbers will now be dealt with in turn for the vader project. They have in common that both profits and capital costs need to be calculated on an accruals basis and in money terms i.e. by reference to the current costs and prices of the years to which they refer.

Given that the real risk-free asset is so drawn up as to appreciate at the same rate as the Retail Price Index, it would seem a useful starting point to forecast the rate at which this index will change over the vader project's life. Here, however, a paradox becomes apparent. The main advantage of indexation is that its introduction eliminates the need to forecast inflation rates correctly by making contractual arrangements which (through the use of indexing clauses) stipulate real rates of interest instead of nominal ones. Thus if it were possible to make consistently accurate estimates of future changes in the Retail Price Index, much of the justification for indexation would vanish. This, though, is more than modern forecasting technology can offer; instead, reliance will be placed upon indexation together with a naive forecast that the Retail Price Index will be subject to a constant 15% p.a. change. Letting the rate of change be represented by p, the forecast is then $p = 0.15$. This constant-rate forecast has no justification save simplicity, and in practice a rate p_j might be forecast for the jth year of the vader project's life, with this rate varying from one year to another.

There can be no doubt that it is extremely difficult to forecast inflation rates. Recently, Logue and Willett [64] have shown that as the average rate of price change increases so the variability of inflation tends also to increase – which implies that as it becomes more important to forecast the inflation rate so it becomes more difficult to do so with a useful degree of accuracy. It may therefore be advisable for management to seek specialist help. A valuable list of sources providing forecasts of inflation, both generally and for specific commodities, is to be found in Shohet and Westwick [89, pp. 29–36].

The mention of inflation rates for specific commodities brings up an important point. It is unlikely that revenues and costs per unit for the vader project will inflate at the same rate as one another. Even if by coincidence their rates of inflation did happen to be equal, this common rate would only by a further coincidence be equal to the rate of increase of the Retail Price Index. Simulations by Edwards [33] and Knutson [58, pp. 32–7, 48–52] have served to illustrate the extreme sensitivity of rates of return and present values to minor movements in unit costs relative to unit prices. That outcomes should be so sensitive is not surprising when it is remembered how often net cash flows represent the small residual obtained by subtracting large cash outflows from only slightly larger inflows. The factors by which outflows and inflows are multiplied to take account of inflation need only differ very slightly from one another for the effect on the *net* cash flows to be very marked.[11]

It is consequently important in capital investment appraisal to take explicit account of forecast relative price changes. This involves the introduction of variables called 'appreciation factors'[12] showing how much a particular price or cost is forecast to appreciate relative to the Retail Price Index. In precise terms, the appreciation factors for operating costs and revenues may be defined as follows:

The appreciation factor for unit prices of output relative to the Retail Price Index is x. (Thus if its value for the project were to be taken as $x = 0.5$, the implication would be that the price per unit for vaders was expected to increase half as rapidly as the Retail Price Index.)

Appreciation factors for the unit costs of labour, materials and expenses are represented by y_L, y_m and y_e in that order. (Thus if the value $y_m = 2$ were to be taken, this would imply a forecast that an index of unit costs for the materials consumed by the vader project would increase twice as rapidly as the Retail Price Index.)

There is no necessary reason why the appreciation factors chosen should relate to the broad categories of labour (y_L), materials (y_m) and expenses (y_e). A more disaggregated approach, with appreciation factors relating (for example) to individual raw materials would be equally possible. However, it seems likely that there will be diminishing returns to progressively greater disaggregation, with successively finer cost categories yielding smaller and smaller improvements in forecast accuracy.

Similar considerations arise when considering whether the appreciation factor for a given item of cost or revenue should be the same from one year to another. For example, it is possible to argue that appreciation factors should follow the undulations of the trade cycle as it affects the industry in which the project is set. This would imply that revenue appreciation factors should exceed cost appreciation factors on the upswing of the cycle, and vice versa on the downswing; the snag clearly lying in the additional complexity of this approach, which must impose a strain upon the forecasting function. As a compromise, one major firm with which this author is acquainted sets appreciation factors which differ between one year and another only for the first two to three years of a project's life, i.e. the time required to move to the midpoint of this industry's trade cycle from whatever point it is at when the project is initiated. After the first two to three years, a single value is assigned to each cost and revenue appreciation factor, to reflect what is forecast to be 'average-of-cycle' cost and revenue behaviour. To preserve simplicity, this sophistication will not be adopted for the vader project, though it has much to commend it.

Here, as elsewhere, the question of how to forecast appreciation factors would benefit from further study. On the revenue side, a separate appreciation factor may be forecast for each of a project's outputs, or a single factor may serve to cover all of them. The vader project has a single output, and Company R's economic staff consider that competition in the vader market will make it difficult to pass on in full cost increases without suffering an unacceptable decline in sales volume and market share. In view of this, and bearing in mind also top management assumptions about the future course of price control legislation, a revenue appreciation factor of $x = 0.9$ has been settled upon within Company R.

The forecasting of cost appreciation factors may be carried out by extrapolating the past behaviour of cost components, then modifying the results in the light of managerial expectations concerning future inflation. In the case of the vader project, consider the forecasting of an appreciation factor for raw materials and fuel. Given that the project has an eight-year duration (1979–86 inclusive) and that vaders fall within the mechanical engineering industry, an obvious approach would be as follows: Go back eight years from the decision date, and examine over the period between January 1971 and January 1979 the movement in a specific price index for raw materials and fuel used in mechanical engineering relative to the Retail Price Index. The required mechanical engineering index is published[13] in *Trade and Industry*, and yields the following comparison:

	Index at January 1971	Index[14] at January 1979
Mechanical engineering	100	233
		÷
Retail prices	100	258
Historic appreciation factor		0.9

This historic appreciation factor relates to the most recent period of length equivalent to the project's duration and prior to the date at which a decision on the project has to be taken. It is not, of course, suggested that this factor should simply be inserted into the vader project appraisal without more ado. Just because y_m has historically been 0.9, it does not follow that the appropriate value for y_m over the period 1979–86 will also be 0.9. (Indeed, when the cost appreciation factor for a good has been below unity, increased demand for it as a substitute may imply that its appreciation factor will soon *exceed* unity.) Nonetheless, the historic value of an appreciation factor represents a basis for judgements concerning its future value. These judgements, as Greer [43] has pointed out, may be subjected to postaudit by computing the actual values of the appreciation factors and comparing them with the forecast values. Thus an error-learning process may be set up, with the objective of generating a gradual improvement in the quality of forecasts.

The same approach to cost forecasting as was used here for materials may also be applied to wages and expenses. Here, however, a constraint should be noted; appreciation factors which differ very greatly from one another or from unity become increasingly unlikely the longer is the life of the project concerned. It is easy to make capital investment appraisals quite unrealistic by extrapolating large differential rates of inflation very far into the future. Rates of price and cost inflation tend over the long run to converge upon one another, in a process described by Wiles [99, p. 385] as follows:

'Product prices rise by moderate amounts independently of demand, and so in defiance of orthodox micro-theory. Moreover, they do so in response not only to wages but to costs in general; so that if a firm delivering semi-fabricates raises their prices in response to its own workers' wage-rise the user of semi-fabricates puts up his prices too, in response to an increase which is to him not in labour but in material costs.'

Elaborating on this, Carter and Voss [24, p. 64] warn that while it might (for example) be sound to assume that wages would rise 6 % faster than other costs for a period of three to four years, the same differential if persisted with over fifteen years might well give grossly distorted and highly improbable results.

This argument should not be carried too far, however, Knutson's [58, pp. 81–4] calculation of 86 appreciation factors for commodities over five-year periods during 1933–63 gave an arithmetic mean of 0.96 but a standard deviation of 0.99, with extreme values at − 1.27 and 3.74. Even taking ten-year periods rather than five only reduced the standard deviation to 0.78, which suggests that the convergence of appreciation factors upon one another and upon unity (as described above) may take effect quite slowly.[15]

Bearing all these points in mind, the central staff of Company R have arrived at the following appreciation factors for application to the operating costs and revenues of the vader project:

$$x = 0.9; \ y_L = 1.2; \ y_m = 1.1; \ y_e = 1$$

Armed with these factors, and with the previously-mentioned 15 % p.a.

increase forecast for the Retail Price Index, the central staff are now in a position to compute the operating costs and revenues on an accruals basis. This will lead to the taxable profits from operations, which are themselves an intermediate step toward computing the tax liability arising from the vader project.

For this project, it will be assumed that sales, purchases and the using-up of inputs to production all occur at an even rate throughout the year. Then for year j, the following definition may be established:

$$h = j - 0.5 \qquad (2-2)$$

Letting sales revenue for year j at current prices be represented by S_{cj}, it follows that:

$$S_{cj} = (1 + xp)^h S_j \qquad (2-3)$$

Similarly, if labour costs at current prices are represented by L_{cj} and expenses at current prices by E_{cj}, these equations may be constructed:

$$L_{cj} = (1 + y_L p)^h L_j \qquad (2-4)$$

$$E_{cj} = (1 + y_e p)^h E_j \qquad (2-5)$$

With the materials bought (at base-cost) in year j denoted by M_{bj}, it follows that the materials bought at current cost in year j, M_{cj}, may be obtained from equation $(2-6)$ below:

$$M_{cj} = (1 + y_m p)^h M_{bj} \qquad (2-6)$$

There is, however, a complication regarding materials costs. In obtaining the taxable profits from operations, materials costs are taken as being recorded on a FIFO basis. For the project under consideration, the relationship between M_{uj} and R_j will be taken as implying that the lag (d) between acquiring an item of material and its being charged out to production is on average three months. Then on an annual basis $d = 0.25$ and the cost of materials used at FIFO for year j, M_{hj}, is given by:

$$M_{hj} = (1 + y_m p)^{h-d} M_{uj} \qquad (2-7)$$

The taxable profit from operations is simply taxable profit before the deduction of capital allowances and debt servicing costs. If the taxable profit for year j is represented by P_j, then:

$$P_j = S_{cj} - (L_{cj} + E_{cj} + M_{hj}) \qquad (2-8)$$

For the vader project, sufficient information has already been given to make possible the calculation of taxable profits from operations using equations $(2-3)$ to $(2-8)$ above. Performing the computation yields the following figures:

$$P_1 = 0 \quad P_3 = 3 \quad P_5 = 212 \quad P_7 = 186$$
$$P_2 = 0 \quad P_4 = 152 \quad P_6 = 226 \quad P_8 = 41$$

Capital costs, just like operating costs and revenues, must initially be modelled on an accruals basis. The resulting figures may then be used as a basis from which to derive capital allowances and grants. In the case of the vader project, fixed capital expenditure is to be confined to plant and machinery. This may be ordered immediately (January 1979) but the bulk of it will not be supplied until 1980 owing to order backlogs at the suppliers. As Brown [19, p. 474] indicates is now increasingly common practice, these suppliers will quote existing prices only as a guide, insisting on charging for their machinery the price prevailing at the time of its delivery. The figures for K_1 and K_2 given by Division Q were at base prices—being obtained from quotations of existing prices sent to the division by the machinery suppliers. They will consequently need adjustment to current prices by headquarters staff before they can be used in the process of capital budgeting. This requires the definition of a further appreciation factor, given below:

The appreciation factor for unit capital costs relative to the Retail Price Index is w. Staff estimates have settled upon $w = 1.25$, implying that unit costs for the vader project's machinery are forecast to increase 25 % faster than the Retail Price Index during the years 1979 and 1980. Given that capital expenditure takes place evenly through these years, the capital costs at current prices for year j may be denoted by K_{cj}, where:

$$K_{cj} = (1 + wp)^h K_j \qquad (2-9)$$

This gives rise to:

$$K_{c1} = 62; \; K_{c2} = 172; \; K_{c3} \text{ et seq.} = 0$$

The process of computing taxable profits from operations and capital costs on an accruals basis has now been completed. But of course capital investment appraisal concerns itself with cash flows not accruals – hence there arises a need to convert these profits and costs into cash flows. This is the task of the next section.

2.6 Modelling operating and capital flows

As in the last section, attention will initially be focused on operating flows. It will be taken that sales are paid for after a lag of s years, while Division Q pays its expenses after a lag of e years. The corresponding lag in its payments for materials will be assumed to be m years, while no lag will be assumed in payments for labour. Letting the cash inflow from sales be C_{sj}, this leads to:

$$C_{sj} = sS_{cj-1} + (1-s)S_{cj} \qquad (2-10)$$

Similarly, if the cash outflow for expenses is C_{ej} and that for materials is C_{mj}, then:

$$C_{ej} = eE_{cj-1} + (1-e)E_{cj} \qquad (2-11)$$

$$C_{mj} = mM_{cj-1} + (1-m)M_{cj} \qquad (2-12)$$

Finally, since labour is not bought on credit, the cash outflow for labour C_{Lj} is given by:

$$C_{Lj} = L_{cj} \qquad (2-13)$$

The operating cash flow C_j simply represents the arithmetic difference between the cash inflow from sales on the one hand and cash outflows for expenses, materials and labour on the other. That is:

$$C_j = C_{sj} - (C_{ej} + C_{mj} + C_{Lj}) \qquad (2-14)$$

For the vader project, Company R's financial analysis staff in conjunction with Division Q have decided that lags between accruals and cash flows are likely to be such that $s = 0.25$, $e = m = 0.17$. The implication of $s = 0.25$ is that three months' credit is typically taken on sales; the implication of $e = m = 0.17$ is that two months credit is typically received on purchases. Since $s = 0.25$, the cash inflow from sales in year j will relate to sales made in the first three-quarters of year j and the last quarter of year $j-1$. Similarly, since $e = m = 0.17$ the cash outflows for expenses and materials in year j will relate to expenditures incurred in the first ten months of that year and the last two months of year $j-1$. Using this information together with equations (2–9) to (2–14) above it is possible to compute a forecast of operating cash flows as follows:[16]

$$
\begin{array}{llll}
C_1 = 0 & C_2 = (10) & C_4 = 86 & C_6 = 214 \quad C_8 = 125 \\
 & C_3 = (33) & C_5 = 170 & C_7 = 213 \quad C_9 = 55
\end{array}
$$

The procedure for converting fixed capital expenditures from an accruals to a cash flow basis is much the same as that outlined above for operating costs and revenues. Fixed capital costs are taken as being paid k years after they are incurred. Since capital expenditure for year j is on average incurred in the middle of that year, the following equation may be derived for C_{kj}, the cash outflow for capital costs in year j:

$$C_{kj} = kK_{cj-1} + (1-k)K_{cj} \qquad (2-15)$$

Because payments are to be withheld for the vader-producing machinery until it has met certain performance specifications, it is estimated within Company R that $k = 0.5$. This gives rise to the cash flows shown below:

$$
\begin{aligned}
C_{k1} &= 31 & C_{k3} &= 86 \\
C_{k2} &= 117 & C_{k4} \text{ et seq.} &= 0
\end{aligned}
$$

This is not, however, quite the end of the analysis of capital flows. There remains to be taken into account the cash inflow from the resale of the plant and machinery at the end of the project's life. In dealing with this, it is necessary to define a final appreciation factor as follows:

The appreciation factor for scrap receipts relative to the Retail Price Index is z. It will here be assumed that $z = 1$, i.e. that the net realisable value of the vader-producing machinery will inflate at the same rate as the Retail Price Index.

As a further simplification for this relatively trivial item, it will be assumed that when the machinery is sold at the end of year $j = 8$ the sale is for cash. Division Q has already established (see section 2.3) that the January 1979 value of the eight-year-old vader-producing machinery which will be left at the end of this project is £19K, i.e. $H_8 = 19$. From this, the forecast cash receipt Q_8 may be obtained using the following equation:

$$Q_8 = (1 + zp)^8 H_8 \qquad (2-16)$$

Substituting in $z = 1$, $p = 0.15$ gives a value $Q_8 = 58$. This, then, represents a cash inflow taking place at the end of 1986.

So much for the derivation of operating and capital flows. The next step must be to map out the cash flows arising from the use of indexed debt to finance the vader project's working capital. The computations required are carried out in the following section.

2.7 Cash flows from debt financing

Discussion of these cash flows must begin by defining W_j as being the change in invested working capital over year j. More precisely, W_j is the sum of year j's change in inventories and debtors minus its change in creditors.[17] Given the financing situation outlined in sections 2.1 and 2.2, W_j represents the change over year j in the requirement for indexed debt to finance working capital. At this stage, it becomes useful to employ a relationship established by Lawson and Stark [62, pp. 32–5] to the effect that:

$$W_j = P_j - C_j \qquad (2-17)$$

As Lawson has pointed out [60, p. 8] the above relationship is an identity, holding irrespective of the method of valuation adopted for inventory, debtors and creditors. The values of P_j and C_j for the vader project have already been estimated, so this identity can now be employed to find W_j. Suppose that, in the spirit of section 2.1, Company R proposes to finance the working capital of the vader project by incurring bank debt with interest and principal both linked to the wholesale price index relating to the outputs of the mechanical engineering industry (within which vader production falls). Let the forecast rate of increase[18] of this price index (q) be 12 % p.a. i.e. $q = 0.12$. Further, following section 2.2, let a rate of indexed interest (i) of 6 % p.a. be paid on this debt to compensate for its default risk, so that $i = 0.06$. Representing the interest payable in year j on the indexed debt financing working capital by F_j it follows that:

$$F_j = i(1+q)^h \left(\sum_{f=1}^{j-1} W_f + W_{\frac{j}{2}} \right) \qquad (2-18)$$

The explanation for the $W_{\frac{j}{2}}$ term in equation $(2-18)$ is that funds borrowed to finance working capital in year j have on average been borrowed half-way through that year and therefore qualify for half a year's interest. Using as an input to equation $(2-18)$ the change in invested working capital from $(2-17)$ above, the interest payable in year $j(F_j)$ may be computed for each year as follows:

$$F_1, F_2 = 0 \quad F_4 = 7 \quad F_6 = 18 \quad F_8 = 14$$
$$F_3 = 2 \quad F_5 = 13 \quad F_7 = 19 \quad F_9 = 5$$

It is next necessary to consider the cash inflows associated with the raising of indexed debt, and the subsequent outflows associated with repayments of debt principal. In every year in which $P_j > C_j$ a cash inflow W_j arises representing the proceeds of the indexed debt raised to finance the working capital requirement. Conversely, when in any year $C_j > P_j$ the working capital requirement drops and there is a cash outflow as some indexed debt is repaid. The principal of this debt is linked to the wholesale price index for the outputs of the mechanical engineering industry, so that if the amount of debt repaid in year j is given by X_j, the relationship may be established that:

$$X_j = (C_j - P_j)^+ (1+q)^{j-g} \qquad (2-19)$$

In equation $(2-19)$, $(C_j - P_j)^+$ stands for $(C_j - P_j)$ if $(C_j - P_j) \geqslant 0$ and for zero if $(C_j - P_j) < 0$. The indexed debt principal repaid in year j is taken as having been raised in year g, where $(j-g)$ year-old debt is the oldest debt still outstanding. This amounts to the use of a FIFO assumption, in which the oldest debt still outstanding is taken as being repaid first. Its operation may be illustrated by supposing that £83,000 of indexed debt principal is repaid in 1986. At the beginning of 1986, £66,000 of debt remains outstanding from 1982, £19,000 from 1981 and nothing from years prior to 1981. Employing the FIFO assumption, the £83,000 repaid is taken as being made up of £19,000 from 1981 and the remaining £64,000 (to make up £83,000) from 1982.

To summarise, the cash flows consequent upon raising and repaying indexed debt may be represented by W_j where $P_j > C_j$ and by X_j where $C_j > P_j$. Years in which W_j is positive are those in which there is investment in working capital, years in which X_j is positive are those in which there is disinvestment in working capital. Showing for each year the value of W_j or X_j associated with it gives rise to the following magnitudes:

$$\begin{aligned} W_1 = 0 \quad & W_2 = 10 \quad W_4 = 66 \quad W_6 = 13 \quad X_8 = 135 \\ & W_3 = 37 \quad W_5 = 42 \quad X_7 = 44 \quad X_9 = 88 \end{aligned}$$

As the vader project draws to a close and working capital is liquidated, the indexed debt will be repaid out of the proceeds of this liquidation. In section 2.1 above, it was assumed that the indexed component of these repayments was deductible against Corporation Tax. To be precise, this assumption involves rendering tax-deductible an amount B_j, where:

$$B_j = X_j - (C_j - P_j)^+ \qquad (2-20)$$

Under current (1976) U.K. tax law the premium on debt redemption B_j would not be tax-deductible. Yet if it were not deductible (while payments of interest remained so) it would be difficult for a borrower to justify raising finance through a loan with an indexed principal.

Rendering B_j tax-deductible is thus a necessary condition for the provision of indexed finance in the manner envisaged here.

Apart from this change, the U.K. tax system at January 1979 when the vader project decision must be made will be assumed to be unchanged from the system in force in 1976. That is, the existing system of historic cost based taxation will be assumed to remain applicable. This preliminary point having been made, it is now possible to go on to consider in detail those cash flows from the vader project which arise through the existence of taxes and grants.

2.8 Cash flows from taxes and grants

On the tax side, the absence from the vader project of any capital expenditures on industrial buildings makes the computation of capital allowances extremely simple. Since all the capital expenditure is on plant and machinery, it all qualifies for a 100 % first-year capital allowance. Denoting, then, the sum of the capital allowances deductible against the taxable profit of year j by D_j, the following figures may be obtained:

$$D_1 = 62; \ D_2 = 172; \ D_3 \text{ et seq.} = 0$$

Having dealt with these allowances, it is now possible to use the material of this chapter so far to define the taxable profit for year j, T_j, as below:

$$T_j = P_j + Q_j - (D_j + F_j + B_j) \qquad (2-21)$$

This equation simply involves adding scrap receipts to taxable profits from operations, then deducting in turn capital allowances, indexed debt interest payments and premiums on the redemption of indexed debt.[19] Carrying out this process gives rise to the following figures for taxable profits:

$$T_1 = (62) \quad \begin{array}{llll} T_2 = (172) & T_4 = 145 & T_6 = 209 & T_8 = 34 \\ T_3 = 1 & T_5 = 199 & T_7 = 150 & T_9 = (35) \end{array}$$

When T is negative (as in the case of T_2) this implies merely that the implementation of the vader project would reduce the taxable profits of that year for Company R as a whole. It is to be assumed that Company R will always have sufficient taxable profits throughout the project's life for a reduction in these profits to lead to an actual reduction in taxes paid.

In order to forecast taxes paid from taxable profits it is necessary to make some prediction about the rate of Corporation Tax which will prevail over the period concerned. Taking the rate of Corporation Tax as

t, the assumption here is that $t = 0.52$ throughout. The increase or decrease of Company R's tax payments consequent upon year j's amount of taxable profits or losses is then given by tT_j. However, no cash flow will take place in year j as a result of that year's taxable profits. The lag between earning taxable profits and paying Mainstream Corporation Tax (MCT) upon them can vary between 9 and 21 months, and will be taken for Company R as being 12 months. Given this lag, if the cash outflow occurring at the end of year j for the payment of Corporation Tax is represented by T_{cj}, then:

$$T_{cj} = tT_{j-1} \qquad (2-22)$$

Equation (2–22) may seem on the face of it to contain a contradiction. The rate of tax in it has been taken as $t = 0.52$; but it has just been pointed out that only MCT is paid with a 12-month lag. What, then, of Advance Corporation Tax (ACT), which is paid within three months of a qualifying distribution? In fact, ACT has been ignored on the supposition that the vader project's net cash flows will not cause the amount distributed in dividends to alter. If this is so, then ACT payments will be unaffected by the vader project's implementation – and can consequently be ignored. All of the 52 % Corporation Tax attracted by the project will come in the form of MCT, so that $t = 0.52$ will be both the Corporation Tax rate and the MCT rate. For a relatively small project like this one such an approach is fairly safe – but ACT payments are unlikely to remain unchanged where a project is implemented which is large in relation to the enterprise undertaking it.[20]

Going through equation (2–22) inserting the values of t and T_j above gives rise to the following figures; brackets denote reductions in Company R's cash outflows for tax arising from the vader project's capital allowances.

$$T_{c1} = 0 \qquad T_{c3} = (90) \qquad T_{c5} = 75 \qquad T_{c7} = 109 \qquad T_{c9} = 18$$

$$T_{c2} = (32) \qquad T_{c4} = 1 \qquad T_{c6} = 103 \qquad T_{c8} = 78 \qquad T_{c10} = (18)$$

Having analysed the impact of taxes, the last part of this section must do the same for Regional Development Grants. The amount of Regional Development Grant receivable in respect of fixed capital expenditure in year j is given by bK_{cj}, where b is the rate of grant currently in force. (In 1976 for a Development Area $b = 0.20$ and for a Special Development Area $b = 0.22$.) However, the actual flow of cash from these grants does not take place until some time after they become payable. The lag involved can be anything between 9 and 18 months – so it seems realistic to assume here that all the grants payable in respect of year j are in fact paid in the middle of year $j + 1$. Denoting the cash flows from Regional

Development Grants by G_{cj}, it is thus taken that:

$$G_{cj} = bK_{cj-1} \qquad (2-23)$$

The cash flows from grants for the vader project (which is located in a Development Area) are therefore:

$$G_{c1} = 0;\ G_{c2} = 12;\ G_{c3} = 34;\ G_{c4} \text{ et seq.} = 0$$

At long last, all the cash flows associated with the vader project have now been computed. What must be done next is to bring these flows together and express them in terms of a summary statistic reflecting the financial desirability of the project. This is done in the next section.

2.9 Constructing the net terminal value

The summary financial statistic chosen for the vader project must of course take into account the time value of money. Given the well-documented drawbacks of the internal rate of return, the choice would seem to lie between the net present value (NPV) and the net terminal value (NTV). Here, the NTV is to be preferred on the grounds that its computation will serve to highlight the crucially important assumption about reinvestment which will now be made.

It will be assumed that the net cash flows from the vader project are reinvested in the real risk-free asset (and therefore appreciate at the forecast rate of increase of the Retail Price Index i.e. 15 % p.a.) The NTV forecast for the project will then represent the surplus expected from investing in the project and using the proceeds to buy real risk-free assets, this surplus being over and above the amount that would be obtained by investing the funds required for the project directly in real risk-free assets from the start. In brief, the NTV will be the additional sum expected from investing in real risk-free assets via the vader project as distinct from investing directly in those assets.[21]

Since it is a riskless reinvestment that is being taken, the effect of this approach will be to consider in isolation the risk of the vader project. It will in fact be separated from whatever risk may be associated with those projects in which Company R may choose to reinvest the vader project's proceeds. This separation may remove a source of confusion. It will also remove the need to forecast those returns that will be available on investments some years hence when cash from the vader project becomes available for reinvestment. The real risk-free asset is an investment opportunity which will always be present, and which will always yield an absolutely certain real return (of zero).

Having elected to compute the vader project's net terminal value, the next question to arise is that of identifying the horizon date to which this terminal value should refer. Suppose that this horizon date is n years hence. Then with a one-year tax lag, n must always have a value one greater than the number of years over which taxable profit is affected by the existence of the project. Looking at the values of T_j above, it will be seen that these run from T_1 to T_9, implying that Company R's taxable profits over a nine-year period will be affected if the vader project is undertaken. Since Corporation Tax is here paid one year in arrears, the existence of this nine-year 'period of effect' must imply that $n = 10$. Put in another way, the very last cash flow associated with the vader project is T_{c10}, implying a horizon date for the project $n = 10$ years hence. It is to this horizon that compounding must be taken in finding the net terminal value; the project would start on 1 January 1979, so the terminal date is 31 December 1988.

One final point must be made before proceeding to compute the NTV. In performing this computation, the 'cash flows to the equity' procedure is to be adopted. This treats debt finance flows on the same footing as all other cash flows, in a way explained by Merrett and Sykes [71, p. 98] as follows:

> In analysing a capital project it should be apparent that we are attempting primarily to ascertain its advantages to the *equity* shareholders. From this it would appear that, in strict logic, we should in every case set out the net cash flows from and to the equity shareholders. In this analysis, the debt which could be raised on the assets of a project would be regarded as an inflow reducing the total capital required from the equity shareholders, and in the subsequent years of the project's life the interest and debt repayments should be regarded as normal cash outflows.

The implication in this case is that the indexed debt raised to finance the increase in working capital W_j is to be treated as a cash inflow to the equity shareholders, while interest on this indexed debt and repayments of principal are to be treated as cash outflows. Bearing this in mind will make it easier to understand the computation of NTV as set out in Table 2.1.

From this table, it may be seen that the NTV of the vader project for the values of the variables used in this chapter is $+£550K$. Investing in the vader project and reinvesting the proceeds in the real risk-free asset will produce, after $n = 10$ years, $£550K$ more for the shareholders than would have been produced had the sums required for the vader project been invested in the real risk-free asset from the start. The conclusion which may be drawn, then, from the Table 2.1 computation is that implementing the vader project would seem financially desirable for the equity shareholders.

However, this figure of $£550K$ is only a point estimate. The standard risk analysis approach would involve obtaining further information by a

TABLE 2.1 Computing the Vader Project's Net Terminal Value

Terminal Value of:	Formula Employed	Result of Computation £K
Net cash flow from operations	$\sum_{j=1}^{n} C_j(1+p)^{n-h}$	1449
Cash outflow for fixed capital expenditure	$\sum_{j=1}^{n} C_{kj}(1+p)^{n-h}$	(747)
Cash inflow from resale of plant and machinery	$Q_8(1+p)^2$	77
Cash inflow from raising of indexed debt	$\sum_{j=1}^{n} W_j(1+p)^{n-h}$	414
Cash outflow for payments of debt interest	$\sum_{j=1}^{n} F_j(1+p)^{n-h}$	(144)
Cash outflow from repayments of indexed debt principal	$\sum_{j=1}^{n} X_j(1+p)^{n-h}$	(371)
Net cash flow associated with Corporation Tax	$\sum_{j=1}^{n} T_{cj}(1+p)^{n-j}$	(267)
Cash inflow from Regional Development Grant	$\sum_{j=1}^{n} G_{cj}(1+p)^{n-h}$	139
NET TERMINAL VALUE (AT 31 DECEMBER 1988)		550

Note
1. For all but two of the above cash flows, the flow in year j is evenly spaced through that year. One of the exceptions is Corporation Tax, which is paid one year in arrears at the *end* of that year. This explains the use of the power $n-j$ instead of $n-h$ in compounding the cash flows associated with Corporation Tax. The scrap receipts for plant and machinery are paid over in cash at the end of 1986 ($j = 8$), and are hence compounded by $(1+p)^2$.

process of sampling from subjective probability distributions for the variables underlying Table 2.1. However, with more than 30 interdependent variables to be forecast over ten time periods, a fully-developed stochastic model would be unlikely to justify the effort required to construct it. There might also be considerable difficulty in devising criteria by which to interpret the output of such a model. This would seem to be a situation calling for the initial application of sensitivity analysis, using the kind of three-step approach outlined below:

(i) Alter the forecast value of each variable in turn (for all years) by an arbitrary 10 % from the value used in computing Table 2.1. This alteration should be in a direction such as to depress NTV, i.e. a downward direction for revenues and grants, an upward direction for costs and taxes.

(ii) Isolate those variables for which this alteration produces a relatively large effect upon NTV.

(iii) At this stage, bring conventional risk analysis into play by attaching a subjective probability to 10 % adverse movements in the critical variables isolated by stage (ii). Where this subjective probability exceeds some threshold value, it may be deemed that there is a need for more information on the 'riskiness' of the project. In this context, particular stress may be laid upon avoiding situations where whole portfolios of projects are dependent upon the same critical variable, since in such a situation it would be quite possible for all the projects to perform badly together.

This last point will be returned to in the next section, as part of an overview of the whole process of capital project evaluation.

2.10 The process of evaluation

The discussion in this section will stem from a judgement by the author, with which the reader is free to disagree. This author considers it presumptuous to try to develop decision models which cover the whole process of evaluating capital projects, and lead to authoritative-sounding rules asserting that an investment *should* be undertaken because it satisfies certain financial conditions. Capital projects are seen as taking such a variety of forms and being placed in so wide a range of contexts that it seems to this author most improbable that mechanical decision rules can be devised to cover all or even most of them.

From this viewpoint, the following statement by Adelson [1, pp. 61–2] seems useful as a basis for interpreting the net terminal value. (It must be borne in mind, however, that his concern was with present value, making it necessary to substitute 'compounding' where he refers to 'discounting'.) Adelson argues as follows:

[Discounting at the risk-free rate] preserves the distinction between 'interest' (which is essentially deterministic) and 'profit' (which is not) that Fisher [34] seemed to want to make. We discount the risky project on the same basis as we would discount a riskless project (interest) but we require the risky project to show a good probability of achieving a return over and above this (profit.) Thus there is no reason why the discount rate used should be the same as the rate historically achieved. That is to say we take as a *basis* for evaluating risky projects the rate of return obtainable on risk*less* projects—not the average return obtainable on other risky projects. We would then have no need of a 'cost of capital' concept. We would, however, require a 'risk-aversion' concept in its place.

It is beyond the scope of this discussion to develop such a 'risk-aversion' concept, and in any case the orientation here is toward *guiding* investment decisions not toward the development of 'decision rules' *prescribing* such decisions. All that need be said here is that if the NTV of a proposed project (upon the 'most likely' assumptions about costs and revenues) is negative, then all other things being equal that project should not be undertaken. A project with a negative NTV is not showing an after-tax return sufficient to maintain the purchasing power of the shareholders' equity (and shareholders can always maintain their purchasing power intact by investing in the real risk-free asset). Put in another way, the negative-NTV project exposes the equity investor to some undiversifiable risk while earning him less than he would have obtained by investing in the real risk-free asset. Consequently, such a project cannot normally expect to meet with management's approval.

There is no difficulty, however, in conceiving of investment projects (such as those of a 'welfare' nature) which will have negative NTVs yet may still be undertaken. Equally, projects may have positive NTVs yet not be undertaken because the size of the NTV is considered insufficient to compensate for the risk involved. It is doubtful whether anything general can be said about the size of the NTV which will be required to offset a given 'amount' of risk – but a few notes in this broad direction may be helpful.

From the start, it must be emphasised that 'risk' in this context has no objective existence – being based entirely on the subjective perceptions of the managers taking the investment decision. Porter, Bey and Lewis have, in [81, p. 639], summarised a great deal of evidence to suggest that managers' perception of risk has little to do with the measure of risk (i.e. variance) normally proposed in the literature.[22] Managers instead seem to have a two-dimensional view of risk, seeing it in terms of:

(i) the downside semivariance, defined as the expected value of the squared negative deviations of the possible outcomes from a point of reference, most conveniently expressed here as an NTV of zero. This semi-variance may be used to measure the risk that an NTV of zero will not be attained – the larger the semivariance the greater the risk.

(ii) the risk of ruin, defined loosely as the probability that an adverse project outcome would prove so damaging to their company as to place the managers' livelihoods in jeopardy.

Information relating to both these aspects of risk could be obtained if Division Q were to submit two sets of figures to Company R's headquarters instead of one. The first set of figures would represent the 'most likely case' for the vader project, and would consist of those figures for S_j, L_j, E_j and M_{bj} shown above. The second set, however, would represent the 'worst reasonably foreseeable case' for the values of S_j, L_j, E_j and M_{bj}. With this second set would go a note indicating in what circumstances this case would arise, and perhaps also the subjective probability of its arising as seen through divisional management's eyes. There would, of course, remain the difficulty that different divisional managers might well interpret 'worst *reasonably foreseeable* case' inconsistently, in ways depending upon their inherent optimism or pessimism. Only continued experience of the individual psychology of divisional managers would be likely to be of assistance here!

On receiving the 'most likely' and 'worst reasonably foreseeable' figures, the central staff of Company R would compute the NTV associated with each one.[23] The difference between the two NTVs would represent an extremely crude first approximation to downside risk, and examination of the more pessimistic NTV would help to indicate whether any 'risk of ruin' could be involved for Company R as a whole. Suppose, for example, that the figures for the vader project turned out to be as follows:

	Net terminal value (£K)
Most likely case	550
Worst reasonably foreseeable case	110

Examination of these figures would show that at worst the vader project could achieve only 20% of its 'promised' terminal value. However, since at worst it would still have a substantially positive NTV, it could hardly involve Company R in sustained loss, still less in any risk of ruin.

Division Q's view of the circumstances in which the 'worst reasonably foreseeable' case would arise might well be of particular value in a portfolio context. Ideally, Company R would like to undertake a portfolio of capital projects in which an unsatisfactory outcome for one project would arise in circumstances which brought a satisfactory outcome for other projects. Then whatever circumstances actually arose, they would be unlikely to cause all the projects to arrive at an unsatisfactory outcome simultaneously. In any normal circumstances, some of the projects would perform relatively badly but others relatively well. This range of project responses to any normal set of circumstances would imply that the portfolio of projects selected had a low relative risk, in the sense of not covarying strongly and positively with *one another*. Examination of divisional views as to the circumstances in which the worst reasonably foreseeable outcome would arise for each project would help Company R's top management (by comparing different divisions' project proposals) to build up a project portfolio with an acceptable level of relative risk.

It should be noted that the focus here is on the covariance of projects with one another, not on the covariance of each project with aggregate stock market returns. The weakness of this latter approach, which has characterised work on the application of the capital asset pricing model to capital budgeting,[24] may best be illustrated by an example. Suppose that a firm finds itself uniquely well placed to undertake a group of capital projects which are expected to yield the market return but whose outcomes will covary strongly and negatively with aggregate stock market returns.[25] Application of the capital asset pricing model would suggest that this group of projects would be attractive to the firm's shareholders, in that they could expect to receive from these projects the return on the market portfolio, yet undertaking the projects would reduce the amount of systematic risk (i.e. the value of the beta coefficient) associated with holding the firm's shares. Here, the point would be that the firm in carrying out these projects would reduce the extent to which its aggregate project outcome (its overall profitability) varied with stock market returns. These projects, unlike the firm's existing ones, would perform well when the stock market was performing badly (and vice versa) thus reducing the systematic risk of the firm's portfolio of projects.

Suppose, though, that the group of capital projects under consideration was also

 (i) large in relation to the size of the firm; and

 (ii) possessed of a strongly positive downside cosemivariance as between the projects in the group. This may be expressed more simply by saying that the circumstances in which one project in the group would perform relatively badly would also cause the other projects in the group to perform relatively badly.[26]

There would in this situation be a clear potential conflict between shareholders on the one hand, and managers and employees on the other. Shareholders obeying the dictates of portfolio theory would be diversified in such a way as to render the risk of ruin inherent in the firm's undertaking this group of projects insignificant to them. But managers and employees would not have the opportunity to hold so diversified an asset portfolio – being highly dependent upon the single asset represented by their job with the firm. Their undiversified asset portfolios would make them reluctant to undertake groups of projects all of which could perform badly together, and which if they did so might well deprive them of their livelihoods. However attractive the group of projects described above was to shareholders, managers and employees would consequently shun them. Of the coalition of participants which make up a firm, shareholders are organisationally remote; managers and employees play far more prominent parts in the bargaining process underlying project selection. Their concern, as has been shown, is with the covariance of projects with one another, not with the stock market as a whole.

In the last analysis, the selection of a capital budget which partially satisfies the diverse requirements of shareholders, managers, employees, government and other participants in the firm is bound to involve a process of judgement. It thus comes as no surprise to find an empirical study by Carsberg and Hope [22, p.44] reporting 'qualitative judgement' to have been ranked highly by managers as a method of capital investment appraisal. No mechanical decision rule, however sophisticated, can ever hope to encapsulate satisfactorily the delicate balancing of conflicting interests which must inevitably take place.[27] All that has been attempted in this chapter is a representation of some of the cash flow consequences which arise when projects are undertaken in inflationary conditions and with indexed loans available.

2.11 A link between planning and control

At this stage, it will be useful to quote the first three items from Williamson's [100, p. 120] list of the characteristics and advantages of divisionalised enterprises:

1. The responsibility for operating decisions is assigned to essentially self-contained) operating divisions.

2. The elite staff attached to the general office performs both advisory and auditing functions. Both activities have the effect of securing greater control over operating division behavior.

3. The general office is principally concerned with strategic decisions involving planning, appraisal and control, including the allocation of resources among the (competing) operating divisions.

Looking at this list makes it clear that the general office of the divisionalised Company R must discharge two interrelated responsibilities. The staff managers in that office are required to supervise the allocation of resources as between divisions, and something has already been said about this insofar as it involves capital budgeting decisions. But the staff are also responsible for exercising financial control over divisional operating activities, about which nothing has yet been said. The process of divisional control is the subject of the next chapter; before starting it, though, a link may be established between the processes of financial planning and control.

This link resides in the concept of 'return to the equity'. The NTV figure (of £550K) computed above represented the terminal value of cash flows to the equity, and acted as a basis for the financial assessment of the vader project. In the next chapter, divisional financial control is to be based upon the related concept of profit to the equity, i.e. profit after the deduction of debt servicing costs. The distinction between the *ex ante* (project appraisal) and the *ex post* (divisional control) thus corresponds to the distinction between cash flows (for the *ex ante*) and accruals (for the *ex post*). This relationship should be borne in mind continuously when reading the next chapter.

3 The Process of Divisional Control*

3.1 Recommendations in outline

The discussion of this and the following chapter is to be set in a more familiar financial environment than was the preceding chapter. To remind readers of this point, transactions from here on are described as taking place in the more contemporary period beginning in January 1977. For this chapter, the working capital of Company R is assumed to be financed by an unindexed bank overdraft of the conventional kind, costing in 1977 15 % p.a.

As was noted in section 1.2 above, the term division is in this book applied only to separately accountable units within profit-seeking organisations. For a unit to qualify as a division, it must be assessed against a financial performance measure involving both costs and revenues. The focus of this chapter is on the design of financial performance measures for divisions. Basically, the object of such design is to find a viable compromise between the following three conflicting requirements:

(i) Every item of revenue and cost going into the financial performance measure should be controllable by the divisional manager.

(ii) Managers trying to maximise their performance as recorded by the measure should be led into activities consistent with the objectives of the divisionalised company as a whole.

(iii) The measure chosen should facilitate the making of comparisons of actual against acceptable performance.

It is assumed that Company R has adopted the Sandilands [83] system of current cost accounting (even though in 1977 such adoption would clearly not be compulsory). This system is structured around operating profit, defined as the difference between sales revenue and the value to the business of the assets consumed. Within the context of a Sandilands

---

* Some of the material in this chapter is adapted from 'Divisional Performance Measurement in an Inflationary Economy', *Management International Review*, vol. 16, no. 4 (1976) pp. 51–9. It is reproduced here with the kind permission of the editor and publishers of that journal.

accounting system, the task to be undertaken is one of designing financial performance measures for Division Q. In doing this, a distinction is to be made between assessing the performance of the divisional manager and that of the division which he manages; a separate measure is to be proposed for each purpose. The return on capital is not to be used as a performance measure for reasons which are no doubt familiar to many readers, but which for ease of reference are reproduced in the appendix to this chapter. Having excluded return on capital, the discussion will proceed from the start in terms of a residual income approach.

The best way to illustrate the proposed approach would seem to involve a numerical example, laid out in the form of a 'profit statement' for Division Q. All the figures in this statement are at current value, referring therefore to £ sterling at average prices for 1977. Sales are assumed to have been made evenly throughout the year, and labour and overhead costs also to have been incurred evenly, so that no adjustment is required to state these items at average prices for the year. Given these assumptions, the profit statement upon which the financial assessment of Division Q and its manager is to be based would appear as in Table 3.1. Imaginary figures have been used for the table's construction, and for the sake of simplicity prepayments and accrued expenses have been taken as negligible and excluded from the investment in working capital.

The detailed rationale underlying the construction of Table 3.1 will be explained in the remainder of this chapter. In brief form, though, the argument to be advanced is that the divisional manager should be assessed by reference to current residual income, while the division itself should be assessed by reference to current residual contribution. To move from the income to the contribution measure requires the deduction of those costs which can be isolated and identified as having been incurred centrally by Company R on behalf of Division Q. They must be avoidable in the sense that if Division Q were closed, Company R would no longer need to incur them.

The income and the contribution measure have this in common: both of them are reached after the deduction of a capital charge. This charge is computed by applying to Division Q's investment in working capital the average 1977 rate on the bank overdraft to Company R, which of course is Division Q's parent. Short-term loans thus finance working capital (as they did in Chapter 2); the reasoning behind this will be explained below.

This emphasis on working capital gives rise to another point. If current residual income is to satisfy requirement (i) above for a divisional performance measure, then the divisional investment in working capital must be made up entirely of items lying within the control of Division Q's manager. The treatment of the working capital investment in Table 3.1 actually implies the following (fairly realistic) assumptions about the relationship between Division Q and Company R:

(i) Company R must manage cash centrally, so that Division Q's

TABLE 3.1 Division Q: Profit Statement for 1977

	£K	£K
Sales		2500
less		
Direct labour	600	
Direct materials (at value to the business)	1200	
Current outlays on divisional overheads (excluding lease payments on fixed assets)	475	2275
CONTROLLABLE OPERATING PROFIT		225
add		
Realisable cost savings on inventory		30
CONTROLLABLE BUSINESS PROFIT		255
Average value of inventories, 1977 (at FIFO)	137	
add		
Average (book) value of debtors, 1977	400	
	537	
less		
Average (book) value of creditors, 1977	165	
DIVISIONAL INVESTMENT IN WORKING CAPITAL	372	
Charge on working capital at bank overdraft rate (15 % of £372K)		56
CURRENT RESIDUAL INCOME		199
less		
Avoidable costs incurred contrally on behalf of Division Q		150
CURRENT RESIDUAL CONTRIBUTION		49

manager is unable to influence the level of the divisional cash balance. This explains the absence of cash from the divisional investment in working capital.

(ii) Division Q's manager must have authority over purchasing, credit granting and the payment of debtors. (Divisional managers do not invariably have all this authority; the consequences where they have less will be explored in section 3.6.)

Having sketched in the recommendations summarised in Table 3.1, the next step must be to go through that table line by line.

3.2 Direct materials costs under Sandilands

Looking down Table 3.1, the first query is posed by direct materials, which appear there at 'value to the business'. This concept is sufficiently unfamiliar in a management accounting context to warrant a detailed explanation. Essentially it is quite simple; the value to the business of an asset is represented by the amount that the business would lose if it were to be deprived of that asset, and immediately took economically optimal action to minimise its losses. Baxter [11] has called the same concept 'deprival value' but this could well serve to mislead. No attempt is made in measuring value to the business to estimate the loss of profits which might flow from actually losing the asset concerned; deprival is notional, not actual. In keeping with this 'notional deprivation' approach, valuations are based upon the assumption that if it would be economically optimal to replace an asset, then that replacement could always be carried out instantaneously and without any costs of disruption.

In applying the value to the business concept, Sandilands [83, para. 210] identified three bases of valuation which could usefully be applied to all tangible assets. These were replacement cost (RC), net realizable value (NRV) and the present value of expected net cash flows (PV). The appropriate valuation basis for a particular asset was then taken as depending upon its economic circumstances in the following way:

If either NRV or PV or both exceeded RC for an asset, then clearly if a business were to lose that asset the economically optimal response would be to replace it immediately. The loss resulting from notional deprivation would be the cost of replacement, so that here value to the business = RC.

If, however, RC exceeded both NRV and PV for an asset, then if it were lost there would be no economic incentive to replace it. Its loss would mean that it could no longer be sold (yielding NRV) or used within the business (yielding PV). The appropriate measure of loss would depend upon which of these alternatives was more attractive, i.e. value to the business = the higher of PV and NRV.

There are only six possible ways of ranking NRV, PV and RC. Sandilands sets out these rankings in para. 218, and applies the above rules (from paras. 214–17) to derive the results shown below. In each case, rankings are given from the top down, and value to the business is circled, so that in Case 1, NRV > PV > RC and value to the business = RC.

Case 1	*Case* 2	*Case* 3
NRV	NRV	PV
PV	(RC)	(RC)
(RC)	PV	NRV

Case 4	*Case* 5	*Case* 6
PV	RC	RC
NRV	(PV)	(NRV)
(RC)	NRV	PV

What, then, is proposed in Table 3.1 is to match against sales revenue the value to the business (calculated as above) of the goods sold as at their date of sale. In fact, inventory represents one of the simpler applications of the Sandilands/IASG principles. This is because NRV and PV may be taken as being approximately equal for all but abnormally long inventory holding periods. If the selling price of an article remains unchanged, the receipts from selling it a few months hence will be much the same as the NRV of the same article now, simply because there is not a long intervening period over which discounting can have a marked effect. Further, the uncertainty inherent in forecasting the PV of an article to be sold some months hence may in many fast-changing industries make its current NRV represent as good an estimate of PV as any.

Where NRV and PV are approximately equal, the symbol NRV/PV will be used to represent both of them. This approximate equality (where applicable) reduces Sandilands' six cases above down to two, these being NRV/PV > RC and RC > NRV/PV. In the former of these cases application of the Sandilands valuation rules gives value to the business = RC, while in the latter[1] the same rules indicate value to the business = NRV/PV. What has emerged here may be recognised as a sort of 'cost or market rule,' its precise form being 'value at replacement cost or NRV/PV, whichever is the lower'. Only in its substitution of replacement cost for historic cost does it differ from the inventory valuation rule employed in traditional accounting.

This new variant on the 'cost or market rule' is not, however, of universal applicability. There are circumstances in which NRV and PV may differ widely from one another, most noticeably in the case of maturing stocks for which PV exceeds NRV, and which may indeed be almost unsaleable in their immature state. For maturing stocks, Cases 3, 4 and 5 above all become possible. Cases 3 and 4 present no problem, leading straightforwardly to valuation at RC, but Case 5 represents a potential source of difficulty. This would involve the somewhat fanciful case of a maturing stock which it was currently uneconomical to replace (RC > PV) but which it would nonetheless pay to hold to maturity (PV > NRV). In these circumstances, the Sandilands rules would point to PV as the valuation base – a conclusion entirely at variance with the tenor of Chapter 2 of this book. Implicit in that chapter were doubts concerning the whole discounting mechanism required to find PV, so it will come as no surprise to the reader to learn that this author has the gravest doubts about the use of PV as an accounting concept. Fortunately, the difficult Case 5 will very seldom arise in respect of inventory – though it is a case into which fixed assets will often fall.[2] The treatment of fixed assets must therefore be the next priority for discussion.

3.3 Fixed assets – controllability of costs and gains

The basic principle of responsibility accounting would suggest that the divisional manager should have charged against him only those overheads which lie within his control. Applying this principle to Division Q, it follows that if the division (e.g.) carries out its own research or supervises its own advertising, then these overheads should be deducted in arriving at the current residual income measure upon which the assessment of the divisional manager's financial performance is to be based. If, however, research is carried out on a group basis or advertising is supervised from the centre, then clearly the overheads concerned arise outside divisional jurisdiction and should be excluded from the computation of current residual income.[3]

The same principle would indicate that current residual income should be struck without deducting any amortisations of sunk costs, such as depreciation. Here, the point is that amortisations of sunk costs are not affected by the divisional manager's choices as to how his division is to operate. Given the centralisation of investment decision-making advocated in Chapter 2, the divisional manager is conceived as having discretion over operations but not over capital plans; hence even the depreciation on a recently-purchased fixed asset cannot really be said to arise from decision-making by the current divisional manager.

If these points are taken and depreciation is excluded from the computation of current residual income, then lease payments on fixed assets must also be excluded. Otherwise, the divisional manager would be placed in the inequitable position of being charged for a leased asset but not a bought one. In such a position, there would be a temptation for the divisional manager to try to influence the lease v. buy decision in the direction of buying irrespective of overall corporate interests.

One objection is inevitably raised when it is proposed not to deduct depreciation in assessing the financial performance of divisional managers. This is that the absence of depreciation will make it possible to obtain additional capital at no additional expense to the division, while additional labour and materials still have to be paid for. Consequently, it is argued, divisional managers will tend to react by substituting 'free' capital for labour and materials, in doing so adopting more capital-intensive techniques than are justified from the point of view of the divisionalised company as a whole. In a sense, this argument is well-founded. If divisional managers were left to make such capital investments as they pleased, this sort of behaviour might well seem rational from their point of view.

However, empirical evidence for the U.K. reported by Tomkins [94, p. 174] suggests that divisional managers only rarely exercise substantial autonomy over investments in fixed capital. This is confirmed by earlier studies from Taylor, Nelson Investment Services [91, p. 339] and Manchester Business School [67, p. 10] which showed that the same lack of autonomy prevailed even at the beginning of the 1970s when the vogue for decentralisation was at its height. Since all but the most minor investment proposals seem normally to require the sanction of top management, it must be concluded that there can only be limited scope for divisional managers to substitute capital for labour and materials on their own initiative.

This insistence on top management sanction is understandable, since as Williamson [100, pp. 138–41] has pointed out, one of the major potential advantages of divisionalisation lies in the possibility of achieving improved resource allocation as between different lines of activity. He contrasts an external capital market allocating resources among functionally-organised firms with an internal capital market allocating resources among the activities of a single divisionalised firm. While the external market cannot make marginal adjustments and has no right of access to detailed management information, on the internal capital market fine adjustments can be made to resource allocation among divisions on the basis of planning and control information incorporating as much detail as is thought necessary.

But for the internal capital market of a divisionalised firm to operate efficiently, the available investment alternatives must be presented to top management for comparison. If each divisional manager is left free to make his own investments, inter-divisional project comparisons cannot occur and the covariance of different divisions' projects will remain unknown. This covariance received great stress in section 2.10, above, and for good reason; as Solomons [90, p. 159] has pointed out, 'The addition of a divisional activity which is in itself quite risky might actually reduce the riskiness of the whole corporate enterprise,' (presumably by having cash flows which covaried negatively with other divisions' investments).

The need for a good deal of central control over capital investments at divisional level was emphasised throughout Chapter 2 and seems to be well established. Evidence summarised by Morgan and Luck [72, pp. 5–6] and King [57, p. 77] suggests, however, that top management may often lack the expertise to vet project proposals with any thoroughness. There is also a suggestion that the outright rejection of a capital spending proposal might be seen as a reflection upon the ability of the divisional manager who put it forward. If this is the case, top management may well confine themselves to making only minor amendments to divisional capital requests. This would leave divisional management with considerable powers of influence over investment decisions, even though they possessed little formal authority.

These powers of influence, when coupled with a financial performance measure which excluded depreciation, could conceivably give rise to unfortunate consequences. Divisional managers will, in the absence of depreciation charges, be anxious to move toward capital-intensive production; this anxiety could lead them to advance capital projects even where they knew these could not meet top management's investment criteria. In support of these projects (the argument runs) divisional managers would submit cash flow forecasts which were biased upwards, feeling sure as they did so that top management would make little attempt to correct these biases.

This is certainly possible, but quite ignores the strong relationship that is likely to exist between the level of capital spending in a division and the level of profits which that division is subsequently called upon (in its budgets) to earn. It is normally impossible to isolate out the net cash flows from a particular project and compare these against the flows which were forecast when that project was authorised. But a divisional manager who deliberately overstated the likely net cash flows of a whole series of projects would face embarrassment when called upon to earn additional profits based on the net cash flows he had quoted. So long as it is proposed to assess divisional managers not upon their absolute level of residual income, but on residual income as a percentage of budget, the danger of their systematically hoodwinking top management seems remote, even in the absence of depreciation.

It will be noted that the profit statement for Division Q omits any mention of holding gains on fixed assets. These are gains which arise when the replacement cost of a fixed asset rises. Suppose, for illustration, that Division Q at the beginning of 1977 owned a machine bought at the beginning of 1972 for £5000, having an expected life of ten years with no scrap value. This machine is valued at replacement cost, which for an identical new machine stood at £11,000 at the beginning of 1977 and £13,000 at the end. In replacement cost accounting, the computation proceeds on the basis that five-tenths of the machine's services remained available during the first half of 1977 (in which time its price rose from £11,000 to £12,000) and four-tenths remained available during the second half (in which time the machine's price completed its rise, from £12,000 to £13,000.) The realisable holding gain on this fixed asset is then given by:

$$\frac{5}{10}(£12,000 - £11,000) + \frac{4}{10}(£13,000 - £12,000) = £900$$

If the implication of Sandilands that replacement cost may be a measure of value is accepted, then what has happened is quite plain. During 1977, the manager of Division Q has held under his authority a fixed asset which has increased in value by £900. Yet this holding gain has been excluded entirely from his division's profit statement. Clearly, this is a matter that requires an explanation; the next four paragraphs endeavour to provide one.

The increase in replacement cost has given rise to a realisable holding gain, yet this gain may not have favourable implications at all for the net cash flows of Division Q. To be more specific, the presence of the holding gain does not imply:

    (i) that the net realisable value of the fixed asset has increased,[4] or

    (ii) that the net cash flows obtainable from operating the fixed asset to the end of its economic life have risen.[5]

In fact, the net cash flows from operating fixed assets may well fall as their replacement cost rises. Suppose, for example, that new firms are trying to enter the industry in which Division Q operates. These new firms will bid up the prices of this industry's capital goods, thus causing the replacement costs of Division Q's fixed assets to rise and generating holding gains like the one above. But once these new firms are established in Division Q's industry, they will compete with Division Q for labour and materials (thus raising its costs) and will sell their products in competition with Division Q (thus lowering its selling prices and reducing its sales volume.) Both of these effects will tend to reduce the net cash flows obtainable from Division Q's fixed assets.

But surely, runs the counter-argument, an increase in the replacement cost of a fixed asset which Division Q already possesses must give it an advantage relative to other competitors not possessing that asset? This is only partly true. Such an advantage will only arise if the economically optimal action for these competitors is still to acquire the asset at its new replacement cost. The more the new replacement cost exceeds the old one, the less likely this action is to be optimal. Once it ceases to be optimal for competitors to acquire the asset concerned at its new replacement cost, then even the 'relative' advantage conferred by the realisable holding gain on that fixed asset disappears.

This last point requires illustrating. Consider as an example a packaging process which can be performed either by a style 1 or a style 2 machine. Suppose that Division Q acquires a style 1 machine, and that as soon as this is purchased the price of a new style 1 machine increases by £10,000, thus giving Division Q a realisable holding gain of £10,000. Division Q will then have obtained an advantage only in relation to those competitors for whom the acquisition of a style 1 machine is still optimal. To take an extreme case, consider a competitor of Division Q (called Firmcomp) which was contemplating buying a packaging machine, and which was indifferent as between a style 1 or a style 2 machine at the old prices. The only effect of the style 1 price increase in this case will be to cause £10,000 of consumers' surplus to arise from Firmcomp's now-inevitable decision to acquire a style 2 machine in preference to a style 1. Thus a holding gain on a fixed asset may not even confer a relative advantage over competitors, still less cause the absolute level of Division Q's future net cash flows to rise.

3.4 The treatment of inventory

After so thorough a rejection of holding gains on fixed assets as a component of divisional profit, it may seem odd to note that Division Q's profit statement includes realisable cost savings on inventory. These cost savings are, on the face of it, akin to fixed asset holding gains. To illustrate their computation, suppose that Division Q held 100 units of a raw material at the beginning of 1977 when its replacement cost was £5.15 per unit, and 120 units at the end of 1977 by which time its replacement cost had risen to £5.75 per unit. Suppose further that two purchases of this material were made during 1977, one of 100 units at £5.30 each and another of 200 units at £5.60 each to give a (weighted) average purchase price of £5.50 per unit. It simplifies the calculation if two fairly standard assumptions are made here, namely:

(i) that the initial inventory was held while its value as measured by replacement cost rose from $100 \times £5.15 = £515$ to its average-1977 value of $100 \times £5.50 = £550$

(ii) that the final inventory was acquired at the average purchase price and held while its value as measured by replacement cost rose from the average-1977 figure of $120 \times £5.50 = £660$ to the end-1977 figure of $120 \times £5.75 = £690$.

Using these assumptions, the realisable cost savings on the initial inventory are given by $£550 - £515 = £35$, and on the final inventory by $£690 - £660 = £30$, making a total for realisable cost savings on this raw material in 1977 of £65.

The parallels between the above procedure and the computation of holding gains on fixed assets are obvious, yet it is proposed to include the cost savings while excluding the holding gains. What, then, are the differences between them? One difference is immediately apparent. Division Q's manager was assumed at the end of section 3.1 to have authority over purchasing, and therefore to be responsible for decisions on how much inventory to hold. If this manager or his subordinates forecast a price increase for a commodity, it is open to them to buy more than usual of that commodity immediately prior to the price increase. Then if the forecasted increase takes place, additional cost savings will be earned equal to the difference between the new and the old price multiplied by the number of additional units bought.[6] Here, the divisional manager is responsible for the forecast, and may reasonably be assessed against its outcome.

It is just as important to forecast movements in fixed asset prices as it is to forecast the prices of inventory items. If, for example, it is predicted that the cost of a major item of plant is going to rise more rapidly than other costs, it may pay to buy that item now, bring forward the timing of the project using it, and thus earn holding gains. However, capital investment decisions (unlike inventory decisions) tend to be made above the level of the divisional manager. Though divisional managers may supply some of the forecasts used in deciding whether or not to acquire fixed assets, their lack of final responsibility for investment decisions renders it inappropriate to credit them with holding gains on fixed assets once these have been acquired. Even if investment decisions were taken at divisional level, only those holding gains relating to a divisional manager's own decisions could really be credited to him; gains from earlier decisions would simply be windfalls deriving from fixed asset price movements that the existing manager did not in any way predict.

Whereas there may be holding gains on a fixed asset in each of a large number of years, cost savings on an item of inventory will tend to be confined to a far shorter period. This is because firms do not normally hold individual items of inventory for as long as they hold individual fixed assets. Now an increase in the replacement cost of an asset can only represent an increase in the value of the division holding it if that increase leads to the division experiencing higher net cash flows than would otherwise be the case. There can be no guarantee that an increase in the replacement cost of an item of Division Q's inventory will be followed by higher net cash flows to Division Q. But if it is not the 'spurious' value increase will correct itself quickly as the item concerned is sold.

This self-correcting process can best be illustrated by a numerical example. Suppose that Division Q has in stock an item with a replacement cost of £60, which is to be sold for £90. There is then an increase in the replacement cost of that item to £80, giving rise to a realisable cost saving of £20. In turn, this cost saving will raise controllable business profit by £20. Given that profit is meant to represent the change in the value of a business over time, the implication of this profit increase must be that there will shortly be a cash inflow to Division Q which will be £20 higher than it would have been in the absence of the increase in replacement cost. Specifically, it is implied that the net realisable value of the inventory item must have risen from £90 to £110.

Either this implication is true or it is false. If it is true, then increasing the controllable business profit of Division Q by £20 was clearly justified (and especially so if the purchase of this item was deliberately timed to forestall the price increase). But suppose for a moment that the implication turns out to be false, and that the net realisable value of this item remains at £90, as it was before the replacement cost increase. Then the operating profit obtained from selling it will be £90 − £80 = £10, not £90 − £60 = £30 as it would have been prior to the replacement cost increase. Clearly, raising divisional profit by £20 after the replacement cost increase was a mistake; but the error has swiftly corrected itself, since the operating profit arising from the sale has simply been recorded as £20 lower than it would have been had replacement cost remained unchanged.

It is possible, at worst, that the replacement cost increase and the sale of the item might take place in different accounting periods, thus distorting the measurement of performance slightly over time. But unless inventory turnover is quite abnormally slow, the accounting periods concerned are likely to be adjacent, thus keeping the distortion to a minimum.

To summarise, realisable cost savings on inventory are quickly tested by the act of sale, and either validated by an additional cash inflow or corrected by a reduction in operating profit. For this reason, realisable cost savings on inventory are included in Division Q's controllable business profit. (More will be said about such cost savings in Chapter 4, where an integrated planning-control system is presented for the purchasing function).

Unlike realisable cost savings on inventory, realisable holding gains on fixed assets are never validated by the act of sale. These gains have been excluded from Division Q's controllable business profit on the grounds that their effect on subsequent net cash flows may be long-delayed and very difficult to measure. This latter is an understatement; it has been shown elsewhere that there exists no defensible way of allocating corporate net cash flows to individual fixed assets.[7] It must as a consequence be quite impossible to tell, for a particular fixed asset, whether or not a holding gain has been associated with higher subsequent net cash flows to the corporation.

Each of the components of Division Q's controllable business profit has now been explained and justified. But the proposal is not that Division Q's manager should be appraised on the division's controllable profit; rather on its current residual income. The difference between these two is represented by a capital charge, related to the cost of short-term finance and levied on invested working capital. This represents a novel approach to a controversial problem, and is discussed in detail in the next section.

3.5 Charging for invested working capital:

(a) *Determining the rate of charge*
As Division Q increases the level of its investment in working capital, it must either increase the amount of interest payments made by the company of which it is a division (Company R) or decrease the amount of interest received by Company R. From the start, it has been assumed that Company R manages cash centrally. In a centralised cash management system, Division Q may either draw directly upon Company R's bank account or draw upon a local bank account which is kept to a constant figure by movements to and from Company R's account. Both of these approaches imply that Division Q will not bear the costs of financing its investments in working capital; these will show up in lower interest

receipts or higher interest payments on *Company R's* bank account.

Since Division Q makes its own purchasing, credit granting and debtor payment decisions, it may be said to control the level of its investment in inventories, debtors and creditors (which have together been defined as making up invested working capital). It then seems odd that it should be Company R rather than Division Q which bears the cost of financing this investment. Indeed, there are dangers inherent in this approach, for it provides little incentive to Division Q's manager to avoid running up an excessive investment in working capital. To prevent such an excessive investment accumulating, it is widely accepted as desirable that Company R should impose an interest charge upon Division Q. This charge would serve to pass back to Division Q the interest costs that Company R must bear as a result of marginal changes in the level of Division Q's investment in working capital. The idea of imposing such a 'capital charge' is not controversial, being shared by Amey [5, pp. 62–3] and Tomkins [95, p. 163], whose views on residual income are otherwise diametrically opposed.

But if Division Q and its manager are to be charged for the controllable investment in working capital, at what rate is this charge to be made? On this question, opinions differ. The original proposal by Solomons [90, esp. pp. 156–9] involved using the weighted average cost of capital of Company R as the rate to be charged, and this approach has more recently been endorsed by Anthony [7, p. 20]. In its favour, it may be argued that working capital is financed out of the same 'pool' of funds as is fixed capital, and therefore that the same weighted average cost of capital rate should be applied to working capital investments as is applied to investments in fixed capital.

Unfortunately, this approach merely involves exchanging one set of problems for another. It is convenient not to have to specify how working capital is financed; it is extremely inconvenient to have to use the weighted average cost of capital. Really, this involves more than inconvenience – no problem in the whole of finance has proved so intractable as the cost of capital computation. In the context of the discussion here, three major difficulties in particular stand out:

(i) To compute the cost of equity capital for a firm, it is necessary to know how the rate of return required by that firm's shareholders is affected by their expectations concerning future rates of inflation. Presumably, the return they require will tend to increase as inflation accelerates, but the magnitude of this effect for a particular firm will depend, as Bradford [16] has pointed out, on a large number of factors. Even Anthony [8, p. 67] has now been driven to admit: 'There is no precise way to measure the interest cost of equity capital . . . . No one has come up with a practical solution, or at least no one has come up with a solution that is accepted by a large number of knowledgeable people.'

(ii) Even if the costs of both equity and debt could be found unambiguously, there would remain the problem of weighting each cost to reflect the proportions of debt and equity used to finance investments in working capital. The 'pool of funds' argument above would suggest that these proportions are the same as for investments in fixed capital, which merely transforms the difficulty into one of estimating *these* proportions. A great deal of energy has been expended on the question of whether the book or the market values of equity and debt should be used to weight their costs, but this controversy has not proved fruitful. The objective has been to obtain weights which correspond to the proportions in which different capital sources are to be used in the future (i.e. the incremental proportions in which finance is to be raised). However, Petry [80], in a recent study of 84 U.S. corporations, has shown that over the ten-year intervals 1955–65, 1956–66 and 1959–69, the proportions in which new finance was raised corresponded neither to book weights nor to market weights at the beginning of these intervals. As Reilly and Wecker [82, p. 367] have recently asserted, 'By showing that it is not possible to modify the weighted average calculations to make [them] generally valid, we provide formal confirmation to the recognized inadequacy of the weighted average [cost of capital] approach.'

(iii) There exists, in any case, considerable doubt as to whether the cost of capital of Company R is an appropriate rate to use in levying a capital charge on Division Q. It would clearly be preferable to use Division Q's own cost of capital – but this would be particularly difficult to estimate since shares in Division Q are not traded so that neither their price nor their systematic risk can be known. Gordon and Halpern [40] have tried to tackle this problem by developing a non-market measure of systematic risk for a division, but have met only with modest success.

These constitute three arguments of principle against using Company R's cost of capital in the computation of a capital charge to be used in finding Division Q's current residual income. As a further purely practical point, the cost of capital would be likely to prove an awkward basis for levying a capital charge, since it would need re-computing every time Company R's share price changed. If instead the capital charge were to be computed by reference to the prevailing rate on short-term loans to Company R, its divisional managers would then be able to predict the size of the capital charge that would follow from a given investment in working capital, and make their decisions accordingly. It would only be necessary to inform divisional managers when the loan rate to Company R changed, which would be a much less frequent occurrence than a change in Company R's cost of capital.

The use of the short-term *loan* rate here depends upon the assumption that Company R is not currently in a position of cash surplus, so that it enters the market for short-term finance as a borrower rather than a lender. If Company R were to be in the position of lending short-term rather than borrowing, then the rate to use in the capital charge would be the rate that Company R received on its loans, i.e. the lending rate rather than the borrowing rate.

The reasoning behind this is simply that the cost to Company R of investments in working capital is represented by the interest receipts foregone or the interest payments made as a result of those investments. *Either* the borrowing rate *or* the lending rate should be used, whichever is the best approximation to the opportunity cost of marginal investments in working capital. For a company which is currently running an overdraft the borrowing rate should be used, while the lending rate would be more appropriate for a company which currently has a positive balance on its (central) bank account. Where centralised cash management is assumed, as here, the rate used in computing the capital charge should be the rate charged or received on the central account, and should change as this rate changes.

It will not always, or even generally, be entirely true to assume as here that marginal working capital investments are associated with short-term finance. But this assumption is certainly not outlandish; bankers are far more likely to be willing to provide short-term finance for working capital investments than they are for investments in fixed capital. It must be admitted that a 'core' investment in working capital will always be required, and that if some way could be found of managing without this 'core' then this might imply that less long-term debt and even perhaps less equity was needed. The concern here, though, is not with the 'core' but with those marginal adjustments of working capital levels which a divisional manager may be able to make without jeopardising the status of his division as a going concern.

This point may be put in another way by saying that a capital charge based entirely upon the cost of short-term finance will not accurately represent the total financing cost which a division by its existence imposes upon the company as a whole. However, *changes* in such a capital charge will represent quite accurately *changes* in the total cost of financing a division arising from marginal changes in the level of working capital investment made by the divisional manager. Thus a capital charge based on the cost of short-term finance will provide a sound basis for assessing the divisional manager's financial performance, but will be less satisfactory in assessing the financial performance of the division itself. When, in section 3.6 below, a measure based upon residual income is used to signal the possibility of closing or expanding a division, this reservation must be borne firmly in mind.

For the purpose, though, of assessing the divisional manager, the critical consideration is the impact of marginal variations in his division's working capital on the central bank balance of the company. This focus serves to justify the 'costing out' of these variations to the divisional manager at the (borrowing or lending) rate in force upon the central balance. If Division Q buys inventory for £100, then this must be paid for by running down Company R's central bank balance by £100, decreasing interest receipts or increasing interest payments on that balance to a corresponding extent. Later, the central balance may rise again as funds are supplied to it from another financing source, but there is no denying that the immediate source of finance for the working capital investment was Company R's bank account, and for the short-term management performance measure under consideration here it is surely the *immediate* source of finance which is the most critical. The divisional manager is more likely to take decisions which are consistent with overall corporate interests if he bears in mind the external opportunity cost of the funds he is using – and the charge for invested working capital is intended to induce him to do this.

(b) Measuring the capital base
Why, then, stop at *working* capital? Why not levy a capital charge on the total amount of net assets, fixed as well as current? In the words of Solomons, if a division 'is charged for the capital it uses, it will have every incentive to liquidate, or to transfer to other divisions, assets which it can no longer profitably use.' [90, p. 155]. The difficulty here, though, is that the imposition of a capital charge on all net assets will make 'profitably use' mean something quite different at divisional level from its meaning as seen by corporate top management. Specifically, it will lead the divisional manager to dispose of assets whose continued operation depresses his residual income, where the retention of these assets in his division would be in the best interests of the company as a whole.

To give a concrete example, suppose that Division Q's manager is considering at the beginning of 1977 whether or not to dispose now of a fixed asset which will stand in his books for 1977 at a net value of £2000. The top management of Company R will not (it is assumed) compel him to retain this fixed asset should he decide that it is unwanted, nor will it charge against his profit any book losses arising on disposal. Applying a rate of 15 % p.a. to the net book value of £2000 would mean that in 1977 this fixed asset would attract a capital charge of £300. Another consideration is that this fixed asset is highly specific, so that if it were sold at the beginning of 1977 all that could be obtained for it would be its scrap value, which is £100.

Now Division Q's manager is interested in maximising his residual income, upon which he is judged. From his point of view, the alternatives are to increase his residual income by £100 by scrapping the asset, or to retain the asset in the hope that doing so will increase his profit[8] by more than the £300 which the asset will 'cost' him by way of capital charge in 1977. Suppose, for the sake of argument, that the best guess of Division Q's manager is that retaining the asset will increase his profit by £250. For reasons that were discussed in section 3.3, depreciation is not to be deducted in arriving at a division's profit, so that this £250 may correspond fairly closely to the additional net cash flow which Company R obtains as a result of Division Q's retention of this asset. Purely as a matter of convenience, the £250 profit will consequently be treated as a net cash flow to Division Q (and therefore Company R) of £250.

The alternatives of asset retention or disposal may be tabulated by taking the more attractive alternative and deducting from it the opportunity cost of the other alternative. In the tabulation below, the 'more attractive alternative' is seen first through the eyes of Division Q's manager and then through the eyes of the (profit-seeking) top management of Company R. Immediately, a contradiction is apparent.

Division Q's manager would see the situation as follows:

	£	£
Revenue[9] from scrapping the asset		100
less		
Profit from operating it in 1977	250	
minus Capital charge on it in 1977	300	(50)
Increased residual income from *selling* asset		150

However, Company R's top management would take the following view:

	£
Net cash flow from operating asset in 1977	250
less	
Revenue from scrapping it	100
Increased net cash flow from *retaining* asset	150

As a result of the capital charge, Division Q's manager will be motivated to dispose of the asset, when it is in the interests of Company R as a whole that he should retain it. Two further points should also be noted. First, the increased net cash flow of £150 from retaining the asset understates the advantages of retention to Company R, since there will be further net cash flows (at least amounting to the scrap value) in years subsequent to 1977. Second, retention of the asset would still not be in the interests of Division Q's manager even if he were not to be credited with the revenue from scrapping it. On these figures, even the absence of revenue from scrapping would not induce Division Q's manager to keep the asset, since his residual income would nonetheless be £50 higher without the asset than it would be with it.

This numerical example is intended to illustrate the fundamental point that a capital charge on the book value of a fixed asset does not measure the opportunity cost of continuing to hold that asset. The alternative to holding a fixed asset is selling it – but unless a capital charge is levied upon a fixed asset's net realisable value it can bear no relationship to the cash inflow foregone by not selling that fixed asset. Thus in the numerical example the 1977 capital charge of £300 represented an amount three times larger than the entire net realisable value of the fixed asset upon which the charge was being levied. Yet the divisional manager had, in seeking residual income, to treat the £300 capital charge as if it were a cash outflow, thus biasing him toward the premature disposal of a specific fixed asset.

By contrast, the capital charge on invested working capital does approximate to the cash inflow foregone (or outflow incurred) as a result of a decision to invest in working capital. This capital charge is relevant to working capital decisions because they are reversible (inventories can be run down as well as up; debtors can be reduced by tightening credit terms as well as increased by easing them). But fixed capital decisions are not reversible – once a capital outlay has been decided upon all that can be recovered by reversing that decision is the net realisable value of the fixed asset that has been acquired.

The root of the above distinction is that for the working capital assets of a profitable company, historic cost will generally fall below net realisable value. Hence the funds raised for working capital assets (to meet their historic cost) can be paid back from running them down and obtaining their net realisable value. But for fixed assets this is most unlikely to be possible – the net realisable value of a fixed asset will normally be quite insufficient to pay back the sum that would have needed to be advanced to purchase that asset (its historic cost). Bankers are quite familiar with this; it seems strange that much of the residual income literature should have ignored it. The result has been that an inappropriate capital charge has intruded into scrap-or-retain decisions for fixed assets. These decisions should depend on cash flow comparisons, so that capital charges which do not represent cash flows have no legitimate place in them.

Mention of historic cost in the previous paragraph raises the need to justify the use made of it in Table 3.1 for valuing Division Q's investment in working capital. Starting with inventories, these appear in Table 3.1 at FIFO, as representing the historic cost inventory flow convention most frequently used in the U.K. But why should inventories be valued at historic cost for the purpose of deriving a capital charge? The object of such a charge is to approximate as closely as possible to the cost of financing working capital. However, the cost of financing inventories is related to the *historic* cost of purchasing those inventories, *not* the current cost of replacing them. Put in another way, the sum requiring financing as a result of an inventory acquisition is simply the outlay made in acquiring it.

Suppose, for example, that Division Q bought on 1 January 1977 an item of inventory for £20, which still remained in stock on 31 December 1977, at which time its replacement cost was £25. Given that working capital was taken to be financed by bank loans at 15 % p.a. throughout 1977, then the cost of financing this item was 15 % *of* £20, i.e. £3 and it is this amount (not a greater one) which should be charged against Division Q.

(c) The accrual – cash flow distinction

Examination of Table 3.1 reveals that debtors and creditors, as well as inventory, are shown at book values in computing the divisional investment in working capital. The reasoning behind this may best be illustrated by a numerical example. Suppose that Division Q sells goods on credit for £10,000 to a customer, who pays for them after an interval of three months. If this sale had instead been for cash, Company R would have been better off to the extent of three months' interest at the 15 % p.a. overdraft rate on £10,000, i.e. approximately £10,000 (0.25) (0.15) = £375. The imposition by Company R of a capital charge of £375 (based upon the book value of the debt) reflects the opportunity cost to Company R of Division Q's extension of credit.[10]

Making a sale on credit does not involve the incurrence of a cash outflow, as does the acquisition of an item of stock. It does, however, serve to postpone the receipt of a cash inflow, which would have been obtained immediately if the sale had been for cash, not on credit. The opportunity cost in the capital charge relates to the interest payment made (or receipt foregone) as a result of delaying the cash receipt to the end of the period instead of receiving it immediately. Since the manager of Division Q has been assumed to make his own credit granting decisions, the length of the credit period must be deemed his responsibility, thus justifying the imposition of the capital charge.

The fact that the capital charge is not triggered here by a cash outflow serves to stress the fact that current residual income is not a cash flow concept. It reflects the performance of Division Q's manager in respect of current profitability, not in respect of cash flow generation. Now in some circumstances (particularly those of adversity) the ability of Division Q's manager to generate cash flow may well prove critical. If these circumstances prevailed in 1977, a quite different form of performance statement from that in Table 3.1 might be appropriate for Division Q's manager.

This statement would show the value at the end of 1977 to Company R of the operating cash flow generated by Division Q during that year. With a central cash management system, operating net cash flows from Division Q will be remitted to Company R as they are received. Once in Company R's bank account, they will serve to reduce the interest paid (or increase the interest received) by Company R. Obviously, the earlier in the year these flows are received by Company R, the more interest can be saved or earned from them. To reflect this, the cash flows received by Company R from Division Q must be compounded to their end-year values using either the short-term borrowing or lending rate, depending on whether Company R is in the market for short-term funds as a borrower or a lender.

It has been established that in 1977 Company R was a short-term borrower, and that the rate for short-term borrowing was 15% p.a. Suppose, for simplicity, that all of Company R's cash inflows from debtors and cash outlays for factors of production took place at the quarter-year ends.[11] Then, again using imaginary figures, an 'end-year cash flow statement' for Division Q could be drawn up, showing the division's contribution to Company R's liquidity as in Table 3.2.

TABLE 3.2 Division Q: End-Year Cash Flow Statement, 1977

Quarter	Cash inflows to Company R from Division Q's sales £K	Cash outflows from Company R for Division Q's purchases £K	Net cash flow to/from Company R £K	Compounding factor	Terminal value of flow at end-1977 £K
1	650	585	65	$\times$ $(1.15)^{0.75}$ =	72.2
2	550	495	55	$\times$ $(1.15)^{0.5}$ =	59.0
3	500	450	50	$\times$ $(1.15)^{0.25}$ =	51.8
4	750	675	75	$\times$ 1 =	75.0
			END-YEAR NET TERMINAL VALUE		258.0

The manager of Division Q could then be assessed upon the value to Company R of the net cash flow his division had generated, which is here £258K. Note, though, that this figure relates to the divisional manager's ability to provide financial resources for Company R, not his ability to earn profits for the company. These two considerations are frequently confused, and the effect of so doing can be just as damaging as confusing cash flows with accruals in capital investment appraisal.

(d) The effect on an investment proposal
Before leaving the subject of capital charges, one final issue must be faced. This relates to the impact of a capital charge upon the willingness of a divisional manager to go through the process (outlined in section 2.4 above) of putting forward capital expenditure proposals to group top management for consideration. Here, as in section 3.5 (b), the imposition of a capital charge on fixed assets will be shown to have potentially dysfunctional consequences.

To simplify matters, consider a proposal to invest £6000 in a fixed asset which requires no working capital to support it, and which has a four-year life with no scrap value. The divisional manager concerned forecasts that owning the asset would give rise to an incremental net cash flow of £1000 in the first year and £3500 in each of the subsequent three years; he also forecasts that the replacement cost of this asset will rise by 25% p.a. Depreciation is to be on a straight-line basis, and is not to be deducted from profit in assessing divisional performance. The divisional manager is assessed upon his residual income, which involves a capital charge being levied on the net replacement cost of fixed assets. For the purposes of this example, the rate of charge will be taken as 20% p.a.

Knowing, in the absence of working capital, that the profit before depreciation derived from this project must be identical to its net cash flow, the divisional manager will be able to draw up a schedule showing the effect upon his residual income of undertaking the project (Table 3.3).

TABLE 3.3 Effect upon Residual Income of Undertaking Investment Project

	Year 1 £	Year 2 £	Year 3 £	Year 4 £
Net historic cost at end of year	4500	3000	1500	–
add				
Unrealised holding gains, computed as in [32, ch. 6]	1125	1688	1430	–
Net replacement cost at end of year	5625	4688	2930	–
Profit before depreciation (= net cash flow)	1000	3500	3500	3500
less				
Capital charge @ 20% of net replacement cost	1125	938	586	–
RESIDUAL INCOME	(125)	2562	2914	3500

This schedule shows the divisional manager to be in something of a quandary. If he decides to put forward a capital expenditure request based upon the above net cash flows, it is very likely that it will be accepted. The internal rate of return of this project is 27%, which compares very favourably with the 20% rate of capital charge used in computing residual income. If this 20% rate is not too far from the company's cost of capital, then this project must appear quite attractive from a corporate point of view.

But if the divisional manager does elect to submit the project to corporate top management for approval, he must in doing so commit himself to reducing his residual income in Year 1 by £125. This he may be quite unwilling to do, especially if he is expecting promotion or transfer in the near future. He may instead elect to suppress the project, an action which is unlikely to be consistent with the wishes of a profit-seeking top management. There is also the point that application of the capital charge has made residual income performance in Year 4 appear more than 35 % better than it was in Year 2 (£3500 as against £2562), when in fact the net cash flow was the same in both years.

For these two reasons, it would appear that profit before the capital charge is a more appropriate representation of the divisional manager's performance than is profit after the charge. The standard objection to this line of argument has already been mentioned, namely that to assess the divisional manager on his absolute profit will lead him to press for permission to undertake any project which shows a profit before depreciation throughout all or most of its life. This objection may be effectively countered by altering profit targets to reflect those changes in profit before depreciation which are expected to arise as a result of implementing a project. In this case, the divisional manager's profit target would be raised by £1000 in Year 1 and £3500 in each of Years 2, 3 and 4. The commitment to raise divisional profits to this extent would be required by corporate top management as a condition of sanctioning the investment project, and recorded by them at the date of sanction.

A cautionary note now seems to be in order. It seems unlikely that a system of divisional performance measurement will ever be devised which is such that *all* projects which are worthwhile financially from corporate top management's point of view will in *every* year of their lives increase the value of the measure used to assess the divisional manager's financial performance. Indeed, the search for a divisional performance measure which always shows a better performance for a division undertaking projects which are financially attractive to the company as a whole, and never shows a better performance in any other circumstances, has been both protracted and utterly fruitless. Having said that, a capital charge which is based upon a guessed figure for the cost of capital applied to an arbitrarily-determined book value is surely likely to move any divisional performance measure away from rather than toward the desirable situation described above. It is on this as much as anything else that the case for a capital charge which is confined to invested working capital, as here, must rest.

3.6 Assessing managerial and economic performance

Current residual income is obtained by taking a business profit figure, all the components of which are controllable at divisional level, and deducting from it a capital charge. On the figures given in Table 3.1 for Division Q the controllable business profit is £255K and the capital charge £56K. If the divisional manager is free to vary the level of his investment in working capital, the size of the capital charge may be said to be under his control. In these circumstances, current residual income may be used to evaluate the divisional manager's performance, and will be especially effective for this purpose if it is compared against a budgeted residual income figure arrived at in consultation with the divisional manager.

However, it will not do to use the same residual income figure for assessing the economic performance of the division as was used to assess the performance of the divisional manager. Before assessing the economic performance of the division, it is necessary to deduct from current residual income those costs which have been incurred centrally on behalf of the division, and which could cease to be incurred if the division were to be closed down. The concern here is only with those costs which the division inflicts upon the company as a whole, and which are associated with outlays of cash. It follows that no element of depreciation can enter into them.[12] Finding the appropriate costs for any division will frequently involve delicate problems of estimation—but it must be stressed that the problems involved are ones of estimation not of allocation. It is not intended that all costs incurred centrally should be allocated as between the divisions; rather that estimates should be made of the extent to which central costs could be reduced by disposing of *particular* divisions.

The sorts of items which go to make up these 'avoidable' costs will vary from one divisionalised company to another, depending on the degree of centralisation adopted. They will arise solely from the provision of goods and services by the central staff to the divisions; these may involve research and development, data processing and advertising as well as technical support on topics ranging from engineering to industrial relations. In all but the rare situation in which the divisional manager is free to 'shop around' for these goods and services (buying them outside if he chooses) the costs of providing them cannot be treated as controllable by the divisional manager. They therefore cannot enter into the current residual income figure upon which he is assessed. But if it is the economic performance of the division as a whole that is under consideration, then these costs must be taken into account. Hence the economic performance measure (called in Table 3.1 current residual contribution) must be struck after deducting these costs. For Division Q in 1977, they were estimated to amount to £150K.

At this stage, one point must be emphasised. A £56K capital charge is deducted in Table 3.1 when computing Division Q's current residual income. The validity of this £56K figure depends crucially on the assumption in section 3.1 that Division Q's manager has control over purchasing, credit granting and the payment of debtors. As Tomkins has pointed out [94, p. 177] many divisionalised companies operate policies which are at variance with this assumption as regards the treatment of creditors and debtors. One consideration here is that economies of scale in data processing may lead to the centralisation of trade credit administration. Tendencies toward centralisation may be reinforced if corporate top management fear that divisions might abuse any autonomy they had over credit policy. It is, for example, conceivable that divisions might try to keep down their capital charges by paying their creditors extremely slowly while pressing their debtors for rapid payment to such an extent as to damage the goodwill of the company as a whole. One way of averting this danger would be for all credit granting and debtor payment to be supervised centrally through the head office, rather than being the separate concern of each division.

If, in the example used here, Company R were to take this point of view, then clearly Division Q's manager could not be held responsible for the level of that division's debtors and creditors.[13] He would be left responsible only for that part of the capital charge which related to inventories, so that in 1977 his controllable capital charge would be 15 % of £137K, i.e. £21K, to leave him a current residual income of £234K. The remaining £35K of the capital charge would take the form of an avoidable cost incurred centrally, and would be deducted with the other avoidable costs to arrive at an unchanged current residual contribution of £49K.[14]

Having arrived at the current residual contribution, the next question is how to use it for the assessment of a division's economic performance. If an assessment is to be based upon a single performance measure, it must necessarily be tentative. Hence the role of current residual contribution can only be to signal when circumstances have arisen which require further and more detailed investigation. Such investigation may focus upon:

 (i) the possibility of closing or selling a division

 (ii) the possibility of devoting additional resources to a division on the grounds that its prospects for profitable expansion are good relative to those of other divisions.

If a division is currently showing a relatively poor economic performance, then this may suggest the possibility of disposing of it by closure or sale. A relatively good economic performance, on the other hand, may suggest the possibility of expanding that division's activities. The absolute value of current residual contribution can hardly signal either possibility; a signal can only be generated when the contribution figure is compared against some yardstick. This has been stressed from the start – but the yardstick to be used in signalling disposal investigations will be quite different from that used in signalling expansion investigations.

3.7 Signalling disposal investigations

First to be dealt with is the question of the yardstick to be used in deciding whether or not to devote managerial effort to evaluating the possible closure or sale of a division. This yardstick will involve the imposition of a capital charge on the NRV of all the divisional net assets together – including fixed assets as well as current ones. As was pointed out both in section 3.5 (b) and in note 12 to this chapter, the cash inflow foregone by retaining fixed assets for one more year may be approximated by the annual interest obtainable on their opening NRV.[15] But to obtain this interest for a division's fixed assets would require them to be sold – an action which is unlikely to be compatible with keeping open the division concerned. Consequently, this interest cannot be charged as an opportunity cost in assessing the performance of the divisional manager, since it will not lie within that manager's power to sell his division's fixed assets in their entirety. Interest on fixed asset NRVs only enters in as an opportunity cost when the closure of the division is under contemplation, thus bringing into consideration the possibility of a complete sale of its fixed assets.

The yardstick for closure or sale investigations can best be illustrated by reference to Division Q. Suppose that the net realisable value of Division Q at the end of 1977 was estimated to be £500K.[16] Suppose further that an investment was available outside Company R at the end of 1977. This investment involved no risk of default (as in a Government security) and offered an after-tax return to Company R of 8 % p.a. From this information, it may be inferred that an alternative course of action would lie open to Company R at the end of 1977, as follows:

  (i) to dispose of Division Q, and realise the sum of £500K
  (ii) to invest this sum in the security above, thus earning £40K (i.e. 0.08 × £500K) by the end of 1978.

It may be assumed as a starting point that Division Q's transactions in 1978 will be identical to those of 1977, thus yielding the same current residual contribution. The adequacy of this contribution relative to the 'sale and reinvestment' alternative above may then be assessed as follows:

	£K
Current residual contribution forecast from operating Division Q in 1978 (as in Table 3.1)	49
less	
Foregone interest on net realisable value of divisional assets at beginning of 1978	40
CONTRIBUTION NET OF MINIMUM OPPORTUNITY COST	9

If the contribution figure on the bottom line above was to have been negative, this would have served as a signal to commence a detailed disposal investigation. Here, attention would have been focused on the net cash flows to Company R arising from the continued operation[17] or sale of Division Q.

It is possible to argue, though, that a small positive contribution like the £9000 here should still trigger off an investigation of the desirability of parting with Division Q. This is because the £9000 is a contribution relative to the *minimum* opportunity cost of keeping Division Q open. The foregone interest of £40K could have been earned without managerial effort and with absolutely no risk of default. Suppose instead that the £500K which could be obtained for Division Q at the end of 1977 were to be invested to earn the highest possible return consistent with bearing no more systematic risk than would be borne by continuing to operate Division Q through 1978. Quite clearly, an after-tax return in excess of 8 % might well then be earned.

Thus the decision rule 'investigate disposal of division if contribution net of minimum opportunity cost is negative' is a conservative one. Conservative, that is, in the sense of setting a relatively low hurdle for a division to jump if it is to avoid having its disposal investigated. This is entirely deliberate. An investigation into the possible closure or sale of a division is a serious matter, and by its very existence may well have adverse consequences upon the morale and behaviour of those in the division concerned. A signal to investigate disposal which is not too easily activated may therefore be no bad thing.

3.8 Signalling expansion investigations

So much for the use of current residual contribution in signalling the need for disposal investigations. What now of its use in assessing which divisions warrant particularly close study because they seem to promise relatively good prospects for profitable expansion? The most useful yardstick here seems to be current residual contribution as a percentage of value added *to materials*,[18] defined as:

$$\frac{\text{Current residual contribution}}{\text{Sales} - \text{direct materials consumed}} \quad \text{as a \%}$$

For Division Q in 1977 this ratio comes out at 3.8 %, being £49K of current residual contribution divided by £1300K of value added to materials (i.e. sales of £2500K minus direct materials at a value to the business of £1200K).

The rationale underlying the use of this ratio is fairly simple. It is derived from the argument put forward by Penrose [77, pp. 44–9] and endorsed by Marris [68, pp. 114–18] that what stops the firm from taking advantage of all the profitable opportunities open to it is the limited capacity for co-ordination of an existing management team.[19] If this is accepted, then the rate of growth of profit is seen to depend upon the ability of management to locate those opportunities which involve the imposition of the smallest amount of additional work upon them per £ of additional profit earned.

Normally, it will take no more managerial effort to purchase £2x worth of materials than it takes to purchase £x worth. But it may well take twice as much managerial effort to co-ordinate the adding of £2x worth of value to materials as it does to co-ordinate the adding of £x worth. Consequently, the 'contribution as a percentage of value added' ratio above will serve to locate those divisions in which a relatively small increase in value added tends to be associated with a relatively large increase in profit. Since the increase in value added per £ of additional profit is relatively small in these divisions, so correspondingly will be the amount of managerial time and effort required to earn £1 of additional profit.

The same principle can also be used at the level of an individual brand or product. Here, however, the numerator of the 'profit to value added' ratio above must be changed. It will seldom be possible to find out what proportion of a division's debtors and creditors have arisen from transactions relating to a particular product. Figures for total inventories by individual product are also unlikely to be available, and even where available may lack meaning since the same item of raw material may be capable of conversion into any of a number of products. This absence of useful inventory figures will mean that realisable cost savings cannot be calculated by individual product, nor will it be possible in the absence of debtor and creditor figures to calculate a capital charge on the working capital tied up in a product.

Thus out of the current residual income figure only the controllable operating profit component seems relevant at the individual product level. At this level, performance is best measured by what may be called attributable operating profit. This consists of sales less the current value to the business of those inputs of labour, materials and overheads which are used up in manufacturing a product and which would not need to be used up if that product were to cease to be manufactured. On the same argument as above, attributable operating profit as a percentage of value added to materials may serve to guide managers to those products which can be expanded profitably and without requiring very large inputs of managerial time and effort.

3.9 Performance measures: summarisation and interaction

For ease of reference, it seems sensible at this stage to juxtapose the different performance measures that have been advocated in the preceding three sections of this chapter:

At divisional level
Method of assessing managerial performance: by expressing the current residual income actually earned as a percentage of the budgeted figure, and comparing this percentage either over time or between divisions.
Method of assessing economic performance for disposal: by computing current residual contribution net of a minimum opportunity cost. This only to provide a first indication of the likely need for further analysis.
Method of assessing economic performance for expansion: by computing current residual contribution as a percentage of value added to materials. This only to suggest directions in which opportunities for profitable investment may lie, not to act as a substitute for capital budgeting analysis.

At the individual brand or product level
Method of assessing economic performance for expansion or disposal: by computing attributable operating profit. If this is negative, then clearly consideration should be given to the withdrawal of the product concerned. At the other extreme, if attributable operating profit as a percentage of value added to materials is relatively large, then opportunities for profitable expansion may be indicated.

This juxtaposition of recommendations does highlight the reliance that they place upon ratio analysis. Managerial performance is to be assessed by current residual income *as a percentage of budget*; economic performance (for expansion) is to be assessed by current residual contribution *as a percentage of value added to materials*. This dependence on ratios must surely involve the same danger as is exposed in the Appendix to this chapter for return on capital—namely that its use may lead managers toward maximising profit relative to another variable rather than profit as an absolute value. Yet there seems no option but to use ratios when comparing managerial or economic performance as between divisions of grossly unequal sizes.

Actually, this 'ratio maximisation' problem may prove much less serious with two ratios in use (one for managerial, one for economic performance) than it is when entire reliance is placed upon a single ratio such as the return on capital. A divisional manager faced with a control system incorporating the two ratios above must perform relatively well with respect to both of them if he is to be rewarded personally *and* see his division regarded as a strong candidate for future growth. What is more, the ratios interact; an artificial 'improvement' in one ratio can be obtained only at the expense of a worsening in the other ratio.

To take an example of this interaction, suppose that a divisional manager were to be induced to substitute materials for labour in his technique of production on the grounds that the less labour was used the less value would be added to materials and the lower, therefore, would be the denominator of the current residual contribution to value added ratio. In terms of maximising this ratio, it might well make sense to go on with such a materials-for-labour substitution beyond the point that was economically justified. But as soon as this substitution became un-economic, it would begin to depress current residual income, thus placing the divisional manager in a position of performing poorly in relation to his current residual income budget. This clearly would be a situation to be avoided, and would deter the manager from making unwarranted substitutions of materials for labour. Similarly, the danger that marginally profitable sales might be refused on the grounds that they would depress the current residual contribution to value added ratio would be offset by the fact that refusing such sales would almost certainly depress current residual income as a percentage of budget.

3.10 Broader comparisons and wider problems

It may be as well to reiterate here a point first made in section 3.5 (a) relative to the capital charge, namely that the orientation of this chapter is toward measuring divisional *financial* performance for a *single* budget period (a year or perhaps even less). Yet short-term financial perfor-mance is only one dimension along which a division and its manager can be assessed. Under some circumstances, it may indeed be of little importance relative to other dimensions. Following Drucker [31, p. 53], a list of 'key result areas' may be drawn up, in each of which a divisional manager must achieve at least a certain minimum level of performance if he is not to jeopardise the continuing success of his division. The nine areas that Drucker suggested concern themselves with purchasing, marketing, production, research, industrial relations, management de-velopment and social responsibility as well as with the procurement of finance and the maintenance of current profitability.

This book has so far confined itself to the last two of these areas, with purchasing to be the topic of Chapter 4. But all nine areas are important – and any divisional manager can achieve a satisfactory level of current profitability simply by neglecting his other areas of re-sponsibility. If divisional managers are assessed solely on the financial measures put forward here they will naturally tend to neglect matters such as training, new product development, customer service, preventive maintenance and other tasks which require expenditure now to create intangible but vital future assets. This tendency will be exacerbated if divisional managers tend to stay only for a short time in a particular job, so that if they follow a policy of sacrificing future assets for current profitability they can expect to be promoted or transferred before the long-term damage they have done to their division's prospects becomes apparent.

The only reliable way to prevent this neglect of the future must be to measure performance in each of a manager's key result areas separately, and look at each in turn when assessing him. A great deal of time and effort has been devoted to the design of performance measures for different key result areas, and there is an excellent summary of pioneering work in this field by Greenwood [41]. Much, however, remains to be done; such contribution as this chapter has made has been confined to the measurement of financial performance at divisional level.

The challenge of the next chapter is to extend this chapter's analysis below the divisional level to the separate assessment of the purchasing and sales functions. Attention is to be focused upon purchasing, partly because it is particularly vulnerable to the impact of inflation and partly because it lends itself well to the illustration of an integrated planning-control system. Having considered (in Chapters 2 and 3) first planning, then control, in relative isolation, it is clearly necessary to bring them together, which is the function of Chapter 4.

This may be the place to note briefly some differences of emphasis between Chapters 3 and 4. Chapter 3 was largely concerned with monitoring investments in working capital by divisional management; Chapter 4 puts a gloss on this by showing that it will not necessarily be optimal for the divisional manager to minimise the size of his working capital balances by holding inventory only for transactions purposes. More generally, Chapter 4 is concerned to look at some of the factors determining how much inventory it is worthwhile for the division to hold under inflationary conditions, and at how, *within* the division, control is to be exercised so that purchasing policy serves both the interests of divisional management and those of the company as a whole.

The reader may well find Chapter 4 more abstract than Chapter 3, in that it is highly dependent on an economic order quantity (EOQ) model which admittedly represents a considerable simplification of reality. This contrast between Chapter 3 and 4 arises from the differing states of knowledge concerning their topics; the phenomena in Chapter 3 are fairly well understood while those in Chapter 4 are not. Chapter 4 must therefore be less ambitious than Chapter 3, and have as its goal not problem-solving, but the provision of insights from rigour into reality.

Appendix to Chapter 3: The argument against return on capital

The argument against return on capital which is most relevant to divisionalised companies is that its use may inhibit divisional managers from putting forward capital projects which exceed the minimum internal rate of return required by corporate top management but which would lower the return on capital of the division. This problem is likely to be particularly acute in respect of divisions which are earning a relatively large profit on a relatively small capital base, and in respect of projects having net cash flows concentrated in the later years of their lives. It is only a slight exaggeration to say that the more profitable a division, and the longer-lasting the benefits of a proposed project, the *less* likely it is to put that project proposal forward if it is assessed on its return on capital. A division with a relatively high return on capital will not wish to jeopardise that return by taking on even slightly less profitable projects, yet a relatively high return on a small capital base may be much less attractive to corporate top management than a lower return on a considerably larger base.

A numerical analysis of the above points may be commenced by considering a division which has a capital (however measured) of £1000K and which earns a net profit p.a. (again however measured) of £300K. Suppose that divisions may submit capital expenditure proposals to top management, which is broadly willing to accept any project which is expected to have an internal rate of return in excess of 20 %. The division under consideration then finds a project which will cost £60K and give rise (at the end of each year) to the following net cash flows:

Initial Cost	Year 1	Year 2	Year 3	Year 4
− £60K	+ £25K	+ £25K	+ £25K	+ £25K

(It is assumed for simplicity that these net cash flows are equivalent to net profit before depreciation, i.e. that all sales and purchases associated with this project are for cash, leaving this project to involve only fixed assets and no working capital.)

This project has an internal rate of return of almost exactly 25 %, and will therefore be likely to find favour with corporate top management if it is submitted to them. But the divisional manager, if he is assessed upon his return on capital, must look at the project in rather a different light. His division is at present earning a return on capital of 30 %, and he will not want to accept any project which would cause that return to drop.

Suppose that the divisional manager predicts that the gross replacement cost of the assets tied up in the project will be £80K at the end of Year 1. The net replacement cost of the assets at the end of Year 1 will be

£80K × $\frac{3}{4}$ = £60K (assuming straight-line depreciation over their four-year life). Replacement cost depreciation on these assets for Year 1 will be £20K. If the divisional manager is assessed upon profit after depreciation ÷ net capital employed, then this investment turns out to offer him a return in Year 1 of only [(£25K − £20K) ÷ £60K] = 8.3 %, and he will certainly reject it. If, on the other hand, the basis of divisional performance assessment is taken as being profit before depreciation ÷ gross capital employed, then the project will offer a Year 1 return on incremental capital of £25K ÷ £80K = 31.25 %, and will consequently be acceptable to the divisional manager.

But the defects of return on capital may still be present even without the charging of depreciation, as will be apparent when a further example is considered. This involves a still more attractive project, having the same initial cost (£60K) and the same forecasted end-Year 1 replacement cost (£80K) but with net cash flows at the year-ends as follows:

Initial Cost	Year 1	Year 2	Year 3	Year 4
− £60K	+ £10K	+ £35K	+ £35K	+ £35K

This project actually has an internal rate of return of 27 %, but even on the basis of taking profit before depreciation ÷ gross capital employed yields a return on capital in Year 1 of only (£10K ÷ £80K) = 12.5 %, so that the divisional manager cannot accept it without depressing his overall return on capital for that year. This problem with projects having cash inflows concentrated in their later years afflicts both return on capital and residual income; but the latter to a much smaller extent. (In this example, if residual income is computed in the manner recommended in Chapter 3, the absence of working capital makes it certain that residual income would be increased in each of Years 1–4 as a result of accepting the project.)

Suppose, as a final point, the division discussed above (which call Division A) is compared with a much larger one (which call Division B), and that their results are as follows:

Division	Capital (£K)	Net Profit (£K)	Return on Capital
A	1000	300	30 %
B	2000	550	27.5 %

For illustrative purposes, it is convenient to think of the difference in size between A and B as being the result of a single large investment (of £1000K) by B, providing a net cash flow of £250K p.a. and moving B from a return on capital of 30 % (£300K ÷ £1000K) to a lower one of 27.5 % (£550K ÷ £2000K). Now if the investment B made with the

£1000K goes on producing a net cash flow of £250K p.a. for more than nine years it will have an internal rate of return in excess of 20 % and thus surpass top management's previously-quoted requirement. However, Division B will have had its return on capital reduced as a result of making the investment. Here is a good example of a situation in which a division is penalised in terms of its performance measure for trying to act in a way consistent with the overall interests of the divisionalised company. Return on capital (however calculated) cannot satisfy the second of the requirements for a good performance measure laid out at the beginning of section 3.1, namely that it should lead divisional managers trying to maximise their own recorded performance into activities consistent with the objectives of the divisionalised company as a whole.

4 The Integrated Planning-Control Process: Purchasing*

4.1 Motives for inventory acquisition

The holding of inventory as an asset is likely to be substantially under the control of the purchasing manager, while operating activities are not. Consequently it becomes necessary to separate out the consequences of inventory holding decisions from those of operating decisions when assessing purchasing performance. Various attempts have been made at this task of separation, of which the most substantial have been those by Bell [12] and Petri and Minch [79]. The advent of current cost accounting has served to increase the importance of this topic, hence its coverage here.

A convenient starting point for the analysis is the assertion in Amey and Egginton [6, p. 583] that inventory, like cash, is held for a mixture of transactions, precautionary and speculative motives. In circumstances of certainty, in which the precautionary and speculative motives disappear, what is left is the simplest EOQ model.

Here, the optimal order quantity Q is given by:

$$Q = \sqrt{\frac{2AD}{HC}} \qquad (4-1)$$

where A = the cost of placing an order.
D = the annual demand in units (assumed to be continuous, i.e. sales are not made at discrete intervals).
H = the carrying cost of inventory as a percentage of unit cost C per year.
C = the cost of purchasing a unit.

---

* Some of the material in this chapter is adapted from 'Holding Gains, Inventory Decisions and the Measurement of Purchasing Performance', *Journal of Business Finance and Accounting*, vol. 3, no. 4 (Winter 1976) pp. 123–142. It is reproduced here with the kind permission of the Editor and publishers of that journal.

Suppose that Division Q of Company R buys a commodity from a supplier and sells it directly to the public in the form in which the supplier provides it, i.e. without doing any further work upon it. This commodity is subject neither to obsolescence nor to deterioration. In addition, Company R does not face binding constraints on available funds, so that Division Q can carry as much of the commodity in inventory as it thinks will prove profitable. Now consider a situation in which Division Q's purchasing manager feels himself able to predict with near-certainty the date of a cost increase for this commodity (as where this will arise from a Budget the date of which has already been announced). The purchasing manager may as a result of his prediction be induced to increase the quantity he orders just prior to the cost increase date—balancing the additional carrying costs of higher inventory against the holding gains that will arise on the extra inventory if his forecast of an increase proves correct. Whether the manager will vary his purchasing policy in this way depends both upon his confidence in his forecast and his confidence that a successful forecast on his part will be rewarded.

This chapter will outline and evaluate a proposal for a performance measurement system which rewards successful adherence to optimal order quantities. In inflation, such adherence must involve the prediction of future purchase price increases and the adaptation of order quantities to increases once they have taken place – prediction and adaptation operating together to form an integrated process of planning and control.

To keep this chapter's analysis tractable, the precautionary motive for holding inventory will be excluded from consideration i.e. both demand for the commodity and its lead time to delivery will be assumed to be certain. The only thing that will vary is the purchase price per unit of the commodity (which will in turn affect the amount of funds tied up in inventory and therefore the level of carrying costs). All the other elements of carrying cost will remain constant, as will the cost of placing an order. Put in terms of equation $(4-1)$, A, D and H will be taken to be constants, while C only will be permitted to vary.

4.2 Inflation in the simplest EOQ model

Suppose that Division Q were to have, at 1 January 1977, no stock at all of the commodity discussed above. This commodity at that date will cost Division Q £20 per unit, and it is known that it will sell at a steady rate of 1000 units p.a. Those items which together make up carrying costs are running at a rate of 25% p.a. of the cost per unit,[1] while the cost of placing an order is £300. In terms of equation $(4-1)$ above, $A = £300$, $D = 1000$, $H = 0.25$, $C = £20$. From this equation is derived an optimal order quantity Q_1 of 346 units, to be ordered at intervals of 0.346×300

= 104 days (the 300 arising since Division Q works a 300-day year).

In the case to be considered, the Budget day is conveniently placed 104 working days from the start of 1977. On that day, the purchasing manager is confident that the cost per unit of the commodity to Division Q will rise. His best guess is that it will increase from £20 to £26, and remain at that level thereafter. The fact that the Budget day is 104 working days from the start of the year means that immediately prior to it the stock held will be zero – which simplifies the argument. Again in the interests of simplicity, it is assumed that the delivery lead time for this commodity is zero, i.e. that deliveries follow instantaneously upon orders.[2] If the purchasing manager's cost increase forecast proves correct, the optimal order quantity after it will be 304 units (a figure derived from equation (4–1) with $C = £26$). This new optimal order quantity is based upon the purchasing manager's *expectations* regarding the cost increase, and will therefore be denoted by Q_{2e}.

Intuitively, it would appear that the best course open to Division Q's purchasing manager would be to purchase a larger quantity than normal (i.e. than Q_1) immediately prior to the cost increase. A study by Naddor [74, pp. 96–100] has shown that the cost-minimising strategy for a purchasing manager willing to act on his forecast of a cost increase would be to purchase on the 104th day (just before the cost increase announcement) an amount Q_m given by:

$$Q_m = Q_{2e}(1 + P_e) + \frac{D}{H}P_e \qquad (4-2)$$

Here, P_e is the cost increase forecast by the manager, expressed as a decimal (i.e. $P_e = 0.3$).

Suppose that on the 104th day the cost of the commodity does rise, but to £28 per unit, not £26 as the purchasing manager forecast. After this increase, the new optimal order quantity Q_{2a} (= 293 units) may be obtained by inserting $C = £28$ in equation (4–1). Had the manager been gifted with perfect foresight, he would immediately prior to the cost increase have ordered an amount Q_o given by:

$$Q_o = Q_{2a}(1 + P_a) + \frac{D}{H}P_a \qquad (4-3)$$

In this equation, P_a represents the 40% cost increase which has actually occurred (i.e. $P_a = 0.4$).

With no further cost increases taking place between the 104th day and the end of the year, it becomes possible to envisage three alternative situations. These, in ascending order of desirability, are:

(i) a situation in which the purchasing manager did not predict the cost increase at all, and consequently ordered only Q_1 (= 346) units on the 104th day at the then-prevailing cost of £20 per unit. This order of 346 units would last 104 days before being exhausted, so that an order of Q_{2a} (= 293) units would be placed on the 208th day. This order in turn would just fail to last out the year, necessitating a further order (again of 293 units) on the 296th day of the working year.

(ii) a situation in which the purchasing manager predicted the cost increase, but did so incorrectly. Here, in anticipation of an increase to £26, the manager ordered Q_m (= 1595) units on the 104th day. At the 1000 units p.a. sales rate, these units would last through the remainder of the year, with 941 units remaining in stock at the year-end.

(iii) an optimal situation (which has not been achieved) in which the manager predicted the cost increase with perfect accuracy. In this situation, he would order Q_o (= 2010) units just before the increase, which would leave him with 1356 units in stock at the year-end.

The consequences of these three situations may be briefly summarised on a historic cost basis as follows:

Incurred during year:	Situation (i) £	Situation (ii) £	Situation (iii) £
Purchasing costs	30248	38820	47120
Carrying costs	925	4441	5796
Ordering costs	1200	600	600
	32373	43861	53516
In stock at year-end	278 units	941 units	1356 units

In looking at the implications of these figures for performance measurement it is necessary to examine the organisation structure of Division Q, within which the purchasing manager must operate.

4.3 Performance implications of purchasing decisions

It has been established that Division Q is in this case buying and selling, but not processing, a commodity. The organisation structure which follows logically from this is one in which a purchasing manager and a sales manager both respond directly to a divisional chief executive. It has also been established (in section 3.1 above) that Division Q is operating the accounting system recommended by Sandilands [83]. One of the properties of this system is that it may be used to segregate operating profits from holding gains. This property may be turned to advantage here where one manager is responsible for purchasing (and consequently for the earning of cost savings on inventory) while another manager is responsible for sales (and consequently for the earning of operating profits). The divisional chief executive may be assessed upon current residual income (as in Chapter 3), and each of the components of current residual income may be unambiguously assigned to either the purchasing or the sales manager, to give a total picture as below:

Manager	*Is Assessed Against*
Purchasing	*Net* realisable cost savings on inventory, i.e. realisable cost savings *minus* the costs of ordering and carrying. (The purchasing manager is responsible for decisions on how often to order and how much to carry.)
Sales	Operating profit, i.e. the difference between the sales revenue obtained and the value to the business of the goods sold at their date of sale.
Divisional chief executive	Current residual income, i.e. operating profit *plus* net realisable cost savings on inventory. (These cost savings are net of ordering and carrying costs, and contained in the latter is a charge for the cost of financing inventory; hence the use of the term residual income.)

At this stage, it is to be assumed that a sales revenue of £30 per unit is obtained throughout for the commodity under discussion. The implication of this is that both the £20 and £28 replacement costs per unit quoted above fall below the £30 net realisable value. In the terminology of section 3.2, $NRV/PV > RC$ so that, by the Sandilands valuation rules outlined there, value to the business for this commodity is given always by replacement cost.

The replacement cost of goods sold before Day 104, 1977 was £20 per unit; after Day 104, it was £28. Operating profit for 1977 is therefore given by $£30(1000) - [346(20) + (1000 - 346)(28)] = £4768$. Since the units bought on Day 1 were all sold by Day 104, the only holding gains which arise are those on the consignment bought on Day 104. As soon as these goods arrived, and before any were sold, their replacement cost per unit rose from £20 to £28, giving rise to a realisable cost saving of £8 on each unit.

Situations (i), (ii) and (iii) in section 4.2 above differ only in the number of units bought on Day 104. This difference is of course reflected in the amount of realisable cost savings earned. For each situation, total realisable cost savings are calculated as below, and net realisable cost savings are computed by deducting from them the ordering and carrying costs tabulated in section 4.2. The computations are as follows:

The Integrated Planning-Control Process

Situation (i): 346 units in store on Day 104, hence realisable cost savings = $346 \times £8 = £2768$. Deducting ordering costs of £1200 and carrying costs of £925 gives net realisable cost savings of £643.

Situation (ii): 1595 units in store on Day 104, hence realisable cost savings = £12,760. Deducting ordering costs of £600 and carrying costs of £4441 gives net realisable cost savings of £7719.

Situation (iii): 2010 units in store on Day 104, hence realisable cost savings = $2010 \times £8 = £16,080$. Deducting ordering costs of £600 and carrying costs of £5796 gives net realisable cost savings of £9684.

Organising the numerical results of this section into the performance measures outlined for Division Q's three managers gives rise to Table 4.1.

TABLE 4.1 Values of Managerial Performance Measures, 1977

	Situation (i) £	Situation (ii) £	Situation (iii) £
Purchasing Manager Net realisable cost savings	643	7719	9684
Sales Manager Operating profit	4768	4768	4768
Divisional Chief Executive Current residual income	5411	12487	14452

This table may be used to highlight the area of potential difficulty in managerial performance measurement. There is plainly no problem in assessing the sales manager; his operating profit 'score' depends simply upon the excess of sales revenue over the current cost of replacement, and the greater this excess for a given physical volume of sales, the better the sales manager may be said to have served Division Q. The problem arises in respect of the purchasing manager. It has already been shown that situation (iii) is the optimal one, for hindsight indicates that had Q_o (= 2010) units been purchased on Day 104, this would have led to the minimisation of the sum of ordering, purchasing and carrying costs. However, the purchasing manager, who is assessed upon his net realisable cost savings, can improve the value of this performance measure in 1977 by buying on Day 104 an amount in excess of the optimal amount, as will now be demonstrated.

4.4 Dysfunctional consequences of current cost measurement

This demonstration requires the creation of a new situation (iv). In this situation, the purchasing manager's forecast immediately prior to ordering on Day 104 is that the price of the commodity is about to rise to £29 per unit. The optimal order quantity Q_{2f} after an increase to £29 had been announced would be 288 units; inserting this in equation (4-2) in place of Q_{2e} with P_f (= 0.45) in place of P_e gives an optimal order quantity for Day 104, in the face of an expected price rise to £29, of 2218 units. Ordering this quantity would entail having a stock of 1564 units left at the end of 1977. Since the actual increase on Day 104 turns out to be from £20 to £28 (not £29) per unit, realisable cost savings for 1977 are in situation (iv) given by £8 × 2218 = £17,744. Against these must be set 1977's ordering costs of £600 and carrying costs of £6483, but even after deducting these the net realisable cost savings are in fact *greater* than they would have been with the optimal acquisition of Q_o units. The explanation for this is simply that the increase in net realisable cost savings in 1977 is more than outweighed in 1978 by the higher carrying costs arising from an opening stock of 1564 instead of 1356 units. This is shown in Table 4.2, from which it may be seen that total net realisable cost savings over 1977–78 are £5404 in situation (iii) and only £5341 in situation (iv).[3]

TABLE 4.2 Situations (iii) and (iv) Compared over 1977–78

	(Optimal) Situation (iii)				Situation (iv)			
	1977		1978		1977		1978	
	£	£	£	£	£	£	£	£
Realisable cost savings		16080				17744		
less								
Ordering costs	600		–		600		–	
Carrying costs	5796	6396	4280	4280	6483	7083	5320	5320
NET REALISABLE COST SAVINGS		9684		(4280)		10661		(5320)

Looking at Tables 4.1 and 4.2 together, it is possible to draw two conclusions about the assessment of the purchasing manager's performance by reference to net realisable cost savings. These are:

(i) that unless comparison is made against an optimal standard established by reference to hindsight, it is not possible to say whether a particular performance in terms of net realisable cost savings earned is praiseworthy or not.

(ii) that the earning of a higher level of net realisable cost savings in a given year is not always to be preferred to the earning of a lower level. The relevant financial criterion for the assessment of a purchasing manager is seen to be the *optimisation* of net realisable cost savings, not their maximisation.

The task, then, is to design for the purchasing manager a budgeting system which compares actual performance against 'hindsight-optimal' standards. Most of the rest of this chapter is taken up with the design and assessment of such a system.

4.5 Comparison against an optimal budget: Forecasting errors

With the benefit of hindsight, it is clear that the optimal strategy for 1977 would have been to buy a total of $346 + 2010 = 2356$ units of the commodity prior to the price increase; 346 on Day 1 and 2010 on Day 104. On the latter consignment, realisable cost savings of $2010 \times £8 = £16,080$ would have been earned. However, not all of these realisable cost savings could have been said to have arisen as a result of the purchasing manager's skill. Stocks were in any case due to run out just before the Day 104 price increase, making it inevitable that cost savings would be earned on the whole of a newly-bought consignment. If the amount purchased on Day 104 had not been increased at all in anticipation of a price increase, $Q_1 = 346$ units would still have been bought, and these would have been in stock when the price increase was (unexpectedly) announced. Thus $346 \times £8 = £2768$ of realisable cost savings would have been earned entirely unintentionally, simply by virtue of the coincidental timing of an asset purchase which had to be made anyway. Consequently, only realisable cost savings in excess of £2768 may be said to reflect the purchasing manager's skill in predicting price increases. The IASG [52, para. 9.30] recognises this to the extent of grouping such 'deliberate' cost savings in with operating profits.

To systematise matters at this stage, it seems sensible to adopt the following notation.

Let c_o be the realisable cost saving on inventory associated with the optimal inventory policy, so that here $c_o = £16,080$.

Let c_n be the realisable cost saving on inventory that would have been earned had a totally passive policy been followed toward forecast price changes, with no stock held as a result of the speculative motive. Here $c_n = £2768$.

Let c_a be the realisable cost saving on inventory actually achieved.

Then that portion of the realisable cost savings earned which may be attributed to the purchasing manager's skill (i.e. that would not have arisen as a result of a passive policy) is given by c_m, where:

$$\text{If } c_c \geqslant c_a, \; c_m = c_a - c_n \qquad (4-4)$$

But if $c_a > c_o$, then the realisable cost savings attributable to the purchasing manager's skill are given by the difference between the maximum value of c_m that could be earned, which is $c_o - c_n$, and the excess of the actual realisable cost savings over optimal realisable cost savings, that is $c_a - c_o$. Thus:

$$\text{If } c_a > c_o, \; c_m = (c_o - c_n) - (c_a - c_o) = 2c_o - (c_n + c_a) \qquad (4-5)$$

The term c_m may be referred to as the controllable cost saving, in that the purchasing manager has the power to control, through the action he takes in anticipation of price increases, the value that c_m takes. If, for example, the purchasing manager either fails to forecast a price increase or takes no action upon his forecast, then the cost savings he earns will be confined to c_n, that is his cost savings will arise solely as an accident of fortune. In this situation, controllable cost savings will not arise, so that the value of c_m will be zero.

However, this is not the end of the story. So far, the argument of this section has been couched in terms of *gross* realisable cost savings, i.e. no deduction has been made for the ordering and carrying costs incurred in earning those cost savings. In section 4.3, Division Q's responsibility accounting structure showed the purchasing manager as being solely responsible for all ordering and carrying costs, yet he does not have absolute control over them. For example, it does not lie within the purchasing manager's discretion to cease purchasing a commodity entirely, since this would ultimately cause the division to cease trading in it. Such a decision could not be made unilaterally by the purchasing manager, requiring at least the divisional chief executive's consent. In fact, the purchasing manager may be taken as operating within the constraint that he must continue to procure supplies of the commodity to meet its (1000 units p.a.) demand until told otherwise. Within this constraint, the purchasing manager may be taken as exercising two responsibilities:

(i) a responsibility to anticipate price changes and to alter quantities purchased accordingly

(ii) a responsibility, once a price change has taken place, to adapt quantities subsequently purchased to the new EOQ dictated by that price change.

The uncontrollable ordering and carrying costs, from the purchasing manager's point of view, are those which would be incurred when following an EOQ policy which is optimal in terms of the price level currently prevailing. Any costs incurred in excess of this minimum (uncontrollable) level must arise either as a result of speculative purchasing in anticipation of future price increases, or as a result of a failure to adapt optimally to the current price level. In our situations (i) to (iv) above, this latter possibility has been ruled out – these situations differing only in the optimality of their speculative purchasing policy by reference to the future purchase price. Optimal adaptation to the current price is shown by the fact that, after the price increase, all new purchases in situation (i) to (iv) were of the optimal size of 293 units, given the new price of £28 per unit. Thus the possibility of failure to adapt optimally does not arise here, though it will be returned to in the next section.

To summarise, the ordering and carrying costs associated with order quantities of Q_1 ($= 346$) units prior to the price increase and Q_{2a} ($= 293$) units subsequent to the price increase may be taken as unavoidable consequences of the divisional manager's decision to continue trading in the commodity concerned. They are therefore to be regarded as uncontrollable by the purchasing manager. These 346 and 293-unit order quantities are precisely those associated with situation (i), thus the situation (i) ordering and carrying costs may be taken as uncontrollable by the purchasing manager and deducted from the total of his ordering and carrying costs to locate the controllable element within those costs. This controllable element of costs incurred may in turn be deducted from controllable cost savings calculated as above to arrive at what will be called the controllable *net* (realisable) cost savings. Instead of simply assessing the purchasing manager on his net realisable cost savings, as has hitherto been proposed, it is suggested that a method more in accordance with the dictates of responsibility accounting would be to assess him on his controllable net cost savings.

Table 4.3 shows the net realisable cost savings for each of situations (i) to (iv) over the three-year period required for the effect of a price increase – anticipating purchase in 1977 to work itself substantially out. Table 4.4 is derived from Table 4.3 by taking the realisable cost savings associated with situation (iii) in 1977 as being the optimal cost savings (so that $c_o = £16,080$, as above). Then the controllable cost savings are derived by the application of equation (4–4) for situations (ii) and (iii) (in which $c_o \geqslant c_a$) and by the application of equation (4–5) for situation (iv) (in which $c_a > c_o$). Further, the ordering and carrying costs associated with situation (i) throughout the three years are, by the argument above, taken as representing the uncontrollable element within the ordering and carrying costs of situations (ii), (iii) and (iv). They are subtracted from the total costs shown in Table 4.3 to leave the controllable ordering and carrying costs.[4] In Table 4.4, these costs are in turn subtracted from the controllable cost savings, the residue being the controllable net cost savings.

When interpreting Table 4.4, the cardinal points to bear in mind are

TABLE 4.3 Net Realisable Cost Savings, 1977–79, Situations (i)–(iv)

	Situation (i)		Situation (ii)		Situation (iii)		Situation (iv)	
	£	£	£	£	£	£	£	£
1977								
Realisable cost savings		2768		12760		16080		17744
less								
Ordering costs	1200		600		600		600	
Carrying costs	925	2125	4441	5041	5796	6396	6483	7083
NET REALISABLE COST SAVINGS		643		7719		9684		10661
1978								
Realisable cost savings		–		–		–		–
less								
Ordering costs	900		300		–		–	
Carrying costs	1086	1986	3208	3508	4280	4280	5320	5320
NET REALISABLE COST SAVINGS		(1986)		(3508)		(4280)		(5320)
1979								
Realisable cost savings		–		–		–		–
less								
Ordering costs	900		900		900		600	
Carrying costs	983	1883	1048	1948	1023	1923	1317	1917
NET REALISABLE COST SAVINGS		(1883)		(1948)		(1923)		(1917)

TABLE 4.4 Computation of Forecasting Errors, 1977–79, Situations (ii)–(iv)

	Situation (ii) £	£	Situation (iii) £	£	Situation (iv) £	£
1977						
Controllable cost savings		9992		13312		11648
less						
Controllable ordering costs	(600)		(600)		(600)	
Controllable carrying costs	3516	2916	4871	4271	5558	4958
CONTROLLABLE NET COST SAVINGS		7076		9041		6690
1978						
Controllable cost savings		–		–		–
less						
Controllable ordering costs	(600)		(900)		(900)	
Controllable carrying costs	2122	1522	3194	2294	4234	3334
CONTROLLABLE NET COST SAVINGS		(1522)		(2294)		(3334)
1979						
Controllable cost savings		–		–		–
less						
Controllable ordering costs	–		–		(300)	
Controllable carrying costs	65	65	40	40	334	34
CONTROLLABLE NET COST SAVINGS		(65)		(40)		(34)

	Situation (ii) £ (a)	Situation (iii) £ (b)	Situation (iv) £ (c)
TOTAL CONTROLLABLE NET COST SAVINGS, 1977–79	5489	6707	3322
	(b)–(a)		(b)–(c)
FORECASTING ERROR	1218	–	3385
Forecasting error as % of optimal controllable net cost savings (i.e. those in situation (iii))	18.2%		50.5%

Note It should be remembered that situation (iii) involves the purchase of the optimal quantity Q_0 on the 104th day of 1977, immediately prior to the price increase. Thus there is no forecasting error in situation (iii), and since situations (ii) and (iv) both involve optimal adaptation to current price levels (i.e. contain no adaptation error) the whole of the difference between controllable net cost savings in situations (ii) and (iv) and those in situation (iii) is attributable to forecasting error.

first that situation (iii) represents the optimal budget and second that any deviations from this optimal budget arise here solely as a result of imperfect forecasts by the purchasing manager concerning the size of the price increase to take place at the end of Day 104, 1977.[5] The performance measure 'controllable net cost savings' is designed in such a way that its maximum value is associated with the situation which hindsight shows to have been optimal, thus satisfying the requirement laid down in section 4.1 that the performance measurement system should reward optimal forecasting on the purchasing manager's part. Here, the optimal situation (iii) has controllable net cost savings for 1977 of £9041, while the corresponding figures for situations (ii) and (iv) are £7076 and £6690 respectively.

Simple inspection of Table 4.4, however, reveals two limitations of the controllable net cost savings approach. First, while the optimal forecast by the purchasing manager does give him the highest controllable net cost savings in 1977, his controllable net cost savings figure would be better in 1978 with situation (ii) and in 1979 with situation (iv). Over the whole of 1977–79 the optimal situation (iii) does give the highest controllable net cost savings, but this is not true individually of either 1978 or 1979. It therefore seems necessary to assess the purchasing manager over the whole of the period affected by a price-increase-anticipating purchase.

The second limitation becomes visible in Table 4.4 when the forecasting error (which in situations (ii) and (iv) accounts for the whole of the difference between actual and optimal controllable net cost savings) is expressed as a percentage of the optimal controllable net cost savings. This expression of the forecasting error in percentage form may to some extent be useful when comparing the performance of different purchasing managers, but its usefulness for this purpose is much diminished by the asymmetry of forecasting error about the optimal situation. Because of the need to avoid the indiscriminate maximisation of realisable cost savings, *controllable* cost savings were computed for situation (iv) by reference to equation (4–5) but for situation (ii) by reference to equation (4–4). This difference in the basis of computation explains why an error of £1 per unit in an upward direction has led to a 50.5 % forecasting error while an error of £2 per unit in a downward direction has led only to a 18.2 % forecasting error.[6]

If the purchasing manager is rewarded or penalised on the basis of his percentage forecasting error, this asymmetry will give him an incentive to make conservative forecasts of forthcoming cost changes, erring on the low rather than the high side wherever possible. Now it may be that other considerations, such as cash flow stresses or the risk of obsolescence, militate against the holding of very large stocks for speculative purposes. In these circumstances, a conservative bias may be desirable in that low estimates of forthcoming cost changes will lead to smaller speculative stocks than will higher estimates. But the existence of this bias in forecasting error recording must not be forgotten by those who use this particular measurement system.

4.6 Comparison against an optimal budget: Adaptation errors

So far, adaptation errors, which are errors arising from ordering an amount other than the EOQ for the purchase price currently prevailing, have not been considered. In the preceding section, the purchasing manager was said to exercise two responsibilities, and it is to short-comings with respect to the second of these (the responsibility of reacting to past cost changes) that adaptation errors relate. To illustrate adaptation errors, it is necessary to consider a new situation (v). This is identical to situation (i), except that in situation (v) the purchasing manager is assessed by reference to the material price variance, i.e. the difference between the actual and standard cost per unit of the commodity multiplied by the amount of it bought.[7]

In situation (i) no cost increase was predicted, thus rendering it logical there to set the standard cost per unit of the commodity at £20 for 1977. On the 104th day of that year, the purchasing manager, still not anticipating a price increase, ordered $Q_1 = 346$ units, sufficient to last until the 208th day. It is on the 208th day that situations (i) and (v) diverge. In situation (i), the optimal policy for a purchasing manager assessed as above upon his controllable net cost savings would be to order the new EOQ for a unit cost of £28, i.e. $Q_{2a} = 293$ units.

But to order this amount would, it transpires, be extremely un-attractive for the manager in situation (v), who must look to the minimisation of his material price variance. It would be unattractive because 293 units, ordered and delivered on the 208th day, would just fail to last out the year, entailing a further order on the 296th day. In all, the policy in situation (i) would involve the purchase during 1977 of $293 \times 2 = 586$ units at the new £28 price, giving rise to an unfavourable material price variance of $586 (£28 - £20) = £4688$.

The manager in situation (v) could do better than that with respect to his performance measure. Indeed, the material price variance-minimising strategy appropriate to situation (v) in 1977 is dictated by the near-certainty that the standard cost for this commodity will be changed from £20 to (at least) £28 per unit in the new budget commencing at the beginning of 1978. As a consequence, variance minimisation implies the buying of the minimum amount possible at £28 in 1977 (since each unit bought at that price in 1977 gives rise to an unfavourable price variance of £8, whereas in 1978 purchases at £28 incur no variance at all). The minimum purchase at £28 in 1977, to leave no closing stock at the year-end, is given by $1000 - (346 \times 2) = 308$ units, incurring an unfavourable price variance of only $308 \times £8 = £2464$.

TABLE 4.5 Computation of Forecasting and Adaptation Errors, 1977–79, Situations (i), (iii) and (v)

	Situation (i) £	£	Situation (iii) £	£	Situation (v) £	£
1977						
Realisable cost savings		2768		16080		2768
less						
Ordering costs	1200		600		900	
Carrying costs	925	2125	5796	6396	931	1831
NET REALISABLE COST SAVINGS		643		9684		937
1978						
Realisable cost savings		–		–		–
less						
Ordering costs	900		–		1200	
Carrying costs	1086	1986	4280	4280	1098	2298
NET REALISABLE COST SAVINGS		(1986)		(4280)		(2298)
1979						
Realisable cost savings		–		–		–
less						
Ordering costs	900		900		900	
Carrying costs	983	1883	1023	1923	996	1896
NET REALISABLE COST SAVINGS		(1883)		(1923)		(1896)

The controllable net cost savings in situation (i) are given by equation (4–4) as zero. Those for situation (iii) may be obtained from Table 4.4, while those for situation (v) are simply computed as the arithmetic difference between the net realisable cost savings in situation (v) and those in situation (i). This yields figures as follows:

	Controllable net cost savings	
	Situation (iii) £	Situation (v) £
1977	9041	294
1978	(2294)	(312)
1979	(40)	(13)
Total	6707	(31)

Situation (i) contains no adaptation error, and therefore the whole of the £6707 difference between total controllable net cost savings in situations (iii) and (i) represents forecasting error. The forecasting error in situation (v) is the same as that in situation (i), so that the excess of total controllable net cost savings in situation (i) over those in situation (v) represents adaptation error. By this reasoning, the error figures emerge as follows:

	Situation (i) £	Situation (iii) £	Situation (v) £
Forecasting error	6707	–	6707
Adaptation error	–	–	31

Here, the performance measurement system is leading the purchasing manager astray, since from a company-wide point of view the cost-minimising policy is to adhere to the optimal EOQ given the new £28 price,[8] as in situation (i). The cost of failing to adjust order quantities to this new EOQ is the adaptation error. To see how this error may be computed and related to the forecasting error, it is necessary to draw up Table 4.5.

In Table 4.5, it is assumed that the manager in situation (v) orders the optimal quantity $Q_{2a} = 293$ units on the first day of 1978 and that all subsequent orders by him are 293 units in size. Thus the adaptation error is confined to that arising from his 308-unit order on Day 208, 1977. Now situations (i) and (v) are exactly alike as regards forecasting, in that in neither case was the price increase from £20 on Day 104 at all foreseen, so that in both cases only 346 units were ordered immediately prior to this increase. It follows that the forecasting errors in situations (i) and (v) must be equal, and therefore that any excess of controllable net cost savings in situation (i) over those in situation (v) must be attributable solely to adaptation error in situation (v). (There is no adaptation error in situation (i), order quantities being immediately adjusted to the new EOQ, i.e. Q_{2a}.)

Table 4.5 shows the forecasting error in situation (i) to be £6707, using the same technique as was used in Table 4.4. It follows that the forecasting error in situation (v) must also be £6707, and that the remainder of the difference between (optimal) controllable net cost savings in situation (iii) and those in situation (v) must be the result of the adaptation error.

The adaptation error (of £31) is small relative to the forecasting error, but only because in the particular circumstances of situation (v) the price variance-minimising strategy did not happen to involve a wide divergence from optimal adaptation. (While optimal adaptation would have dictated an order quantity of 293 units, price variance minimisation dictated 308 units; the difference is only 15.) In other circumstances, the adaptation error inherent in a price variance-minimising strategy could well be much larger.

What does come out very clearly from these comments is the fundamental inadequacy of the material price variance as a control tool in inflation. As shown above, the minimisation of this variance may well lead the purchasing manager to buy in suboptimal order quantities. The variance also fails to distinguish between forecasting and adaptation errors, which may well be a matter of some importance. For example, it is quite possible that the purchasing manager may rely upon forecasts of commodity prices provided by a corporate economist when deciding whether or not to hold stock speculatively, in which case the forecasting error would be substantially the responsibility of that corporate economist while the purchasing manager remained responsible for minimising the adaptation error. The single figure of the material price variance is, of course, incapable of being subdivided to reflect such a discrimination.

4.7 Forecasting and adaptation errors: Inventory flow problems

The operations in Tables 4.3, 4.4 and 4.5 may be systematised and extended into the following procedures for calculating forecasting and adaptation errors in a period in which an item purchased has increased in price:

(i) Compute the optimal controllable net cost savings for the budget period concerned. Subtract from these the controllable net cost savings that would have been earned had the actual order quantities been purchased prior to the price increase, but optimal order quantities at all times thereafter. The figure remaining represents the forecasting error.

(ii) Compute, for this budget period, the controllable net cost savings actually earned. Compare these against the controllable net cost savings that would have been earned with the price increase forecast actually made, but with optimal adaptation of order quantities to the new price announced. The excess of these 'actual forecast, optimal adaptation' controllable net cost savings over those actually earned represents the adaptation error.

To see these procedures in full operation, it is necessary to look at a situation in which attempts are made to forecast a purchase price increase and to adapt to the increase which actually takes place, but both these attempts fall short of optimality. None of situations (i)–(v) falls into this category (in situations (i), (ii) and (iv) adaptation is perfect; in situation (iii) both forecasting and adaptation are perfect; in situation (v) adaptation is admittedly imperfect, but forecasting is not attempted.) Reluctantly, the need must be faced to create a new situation (vi).

This situation (vi) may at first glance seem a trifle odd. In it, the purchasing manager forecasts an increase in the commodity's cost to £21 per unit and as a consequence buys on Day 104, 1977 the optimal order quantity in the face of this expected 5 % increase. Putting $P_e = 0.05$ in equation (4–2) gives an optimal quantity to be bought of 555 units. In reality, the increase is to £28, not £21, and the consignment bought on Day 104 fails to last out the year, being exhausted on Day 270. At this time, after the price increase and with no new increase foreseen, the purchasing manager proceeds to buy $Q_o = 2010$ units. (An explanation for this apparently eccentric behaviour follows.) This very large consignment lasts through 1978 and is only exhausted on Day 273, 1979. A new order of the optimal quantity $Q_{2a} = 293$ units follows, which lasts out the remainder of 1978.

With 555 freshly-bought units in stock at the time of the price increase,

Table 4.6 Computation of Forecasting and Adaptation Errors, 1977–79, Situations (vi) and (vi)a

	Situation (vi)		Situation (vi)a		Situation (iii)	
	£	£	£	£	£	£
1977						
Controllable cost savings		1672		1672		13312
less						
Controllable ordering costs	(300)		(300)		(600)	
Controllable carrying costs	1503	1203	313	13	4871	4271
CONTROLLABLE NET COST SAVINGS		469		1659		9041
1978						
Controllable cost savings		–		–		–
less						
Controllable ordering costs	(900)		–		(900)	
Controllable carrying costs	8791	7891	(72)	(72)	3194	2294
CONTROLLABLE NET COST SAVINGS		(7891)		72		(2294)
1979						
Controllable cost savings		–		–		–
less						
Controllable ordering costs	(600)		300		–	
Controllable carrying costs	1922	1322	83	383	40	40
CONTROLLABLE NET COST SAVINGS		(1322)		(383)		(40)

	Situation (vi)	Situation (vi)a	Situation (iii)
	£	£	£
	(a)	(b)	(c)
TOTAL CONTROLLABLE NET COST SAVINGS, 1977–79	(8744)	1348	6707

ADAPTATION
ERROR 　　= actual forecast, optimal adaptation–actual forecast, actual adaptation
　　　　　= difference between controllable net cost savings in situations (vi)a and (vi), i.e. (b)–(a)
　　　　　= £10,092

FORECASTING
ERROR 　　= optimal forecast, optimal adaptation–actual forecast, optimal adaptation
　　　　　= difference between controllable net cost savings in situations (vi)a and (iii) i.e. (c)–(b)
　　　　　= £5359

Note The controllable net cost savings for situations (vi) and (vi)a were computed according to the methods employed in Tables 4.3 and 4.4, while those for situation (iii) were derived directly from Table 4.4.

the realisable cost savings accruing from 1977's purchases are 555 ($£28 - £20$) = $£4440$. Taking these realisable cost savings, together with the ordering and carrying costs for 1977–79, data may be drawn up for situation (vi) as in Table 4.6. From this data, the forecasting and adaptation errors must be computed.

The first step in doing this is to generate a modified situation (vi)a, in which 555 units are bought on Day 104, 1977 as above, but on Day 270 of that year and at subsequent order times the optimal quantity Q_{2a} for the new price of $£28$ is ordered. Comparison between situations (vi) and (vi)a will yield the adaptation error, since in situation (vi)a adaptation is optimal whereas in situation (vi) (the actual situation) it is not.

The second step is to compare situation (vi)a with situation (iii), knowing that situation (iii) represents both optimal forecasting and optimal adaptation. Both situations are optimal in respect of adaptation, so that the difference between them may be attributed solely to the forecasting error (which is of course the same in situation (vi)a as it is in situation (vi)).

These two steps are shown beneath Table 4.6, and the result obtained indicates an adaptation error which at $£10,092$ exceeds the forecasting error of $£5359$. Thus it would seem that the downfall of the purchasing manager in situation (vi) has arisen mainly from his poor adaptation of order quantities subsequent to the price increase, and specifically from his curious purchase of 2010 units on Day 270, 1977. Yet under certain circumstances such a purchase could in fact lead to the appearance of excellent performance on that manager's part.

The key to this apparent paradox lies in the distortions which may be introduced by inventory flow assumptions. At the beginning of section 4.2, certain, constant demand together with a known lead time to delivery (of zero) was assumed, from which it follows that existing inventory will always be exhausted at the exact moment when a new delivery arrives. As a result, there can be no need to make inventory flow assumptions, since each item sold may be identified unambiguously with a particular consignment purchased. However, so clear an identification is normally impossible in reality, hence the need for some form of inventory flow assumption.

The flow assumption associated with Sandilands [83, paras. 594–605] and endorsed by the IASG [52, pp. 136–142] may be represented symbolically as follows. Let:

R_{fj} be the historic cost of opening inventory on a FIFO basis for year j.

R_{gj} be the historic cost of closing inventory on a FIFO basis for year j. (It will of course be true that $R_{gj} = R_{fj+1}$.)

J_{bj} be the cost per unit of opening inventory prevailing at the beginning of year j.

J_{cj} be the cost per unit of closing inventory prevailing at the end of year j.

J_{aj} be the average cost per unit of inventory prevailing during year j. Then the realisable holding gains on inventory for year j are given by G_{hj}, where:

$$G_{hj} = (R_{gj} - R_{fj}) - \left(R_{gj} \cdot \frac{J_{aj}}{J_{cj}} - R_{fj} \cdot \frac{J_{aj}}{J_{bj}} \right) \qquad (4-6)$$

TABLE 4.7 Managerial Performance Measures on the Sandilands Inventory Flow Assumption

	Situation (vi) £	Situation (vi)a £
1977		
Operating profit	4476	8037
Net realisable cost savings	1404	(967)
Current residual income	5880	7070
Controllable net cost savings	761	(1610)
1978		
Operating profit	2000	2000
Net realisable cost savings	(9877)	(1914)
Current residual income	(7877)	86
Controllable net cost savings	(7891)	72
1979		
Operating profit	2000	2000
Net realisable cost savings	(3205)	(2266)
Current residual income	(1205)	(266)
Controllable net cost savings	(1322)	(383)
TOTAL OPERATING PROFIT, 1977–79	8476	12037
TOTAL CURRENT RESIDUAL INCOME, 1977–79	(3202)	6890
TOTAL CONTROLLABLE NET COST SAVINGS, 1977–79	(8452)	(1921)

Note that the only circumstance in which one of these performance measures shows a higher value for situation (vi) than situation (vi)a is associated with realisable cost savings in 1977. A purchasing manager, assessed as here upon his controllable net cost savings, will be recorded as achieving a 'better' performance if in 1977 he gravitates toward situation (vi) not situation (vi)a.

When this inventory flow assumption is applied to the data in situations (vi) and (vi)a, with a sales revenue of £30 per unit assumed as before throughout 1977–79, results are obtained as in Table 4.7.

These Table 4.7 results clearly present something of a problem. Notwithstanding the manifest superiority of situation (vi)a over situation (vi), as exhibited in Table 4.6, it would appear from Table 4.7 to be in the interests of the purchasing manager to aim for situation (vi) in 1977 (though situation (vi)a would still be preferable for him over the long run represented by 1977–79 taken together). If he is contemplating immediate promotion or transfer, the purchasing manager is unlikely to be interested in the long run, and will instead focus upon his 1977 performance. In these circumstances, there will clearly be a strong temptation to purchase $Q_0 = 2010$ units on Day 270, 1977, despite the economic irrationality of this from the point of view of Division Q as a whole.

Since the cause of this problem lies in the inventory flow assumption, it is plain that its solution must involve changing that assumption. Recently, Davidson and Weil [29] in commenting upon an earlier paper by Petri [78] have proposed using end-of-period unit costs as an alternative to the average-of-period unit costs employed in Table 4.7. Their proposal may be reduced to two formulae as follows:

Cost of goods sold = (Units in opening stock + Units purchased − Units in closing stock) × Price at end of period.

Realisable cost saving = (Units in opening stock + Units purchased) × Price at end of period − (Units in opening stock × Price at beginning of period + Units purchased × Price at which purchased.)

These formulae, when applied to situations (vi) and (vi)a in 1977,[9] split up the current residual income differently as between operating profit and cost savings compared to the split in Table 4.7. The results obtained are as follows:

	Situation (vi) £	Situation (vi)a £
Operating profit	2000	2000
Net realisable cost savings	3880	5070
Current residual income	5880	7070
Controllable net cost savings	3237	4427

Here, controllable net cost savings are greater in situation (vi)a than in situation (vi). This is the reverse of the situation in Table 4.7, and indicates that application of the Davidson-Weil formulae has removed the incentive to stock up after a price increase which was implicit in the

Sandilands inventory flow assumption. There is, however, a drawback to offset against this advantage. The operating profit figure derived from the application of the Davidson-Weil formulae involves a comparison between sales revenue stated at *average* selling prices for the year and cost of sales stated in terms of *end-of-year* purchase prices. The result, in inflation, of this comparison of unlike magnitudes is to depress operating profit artificially, thereby reducing its usefulness for reporting purposes and as a measure of how much may be distributed while maintaining physical capital intact.[10]

It would, of course, be possible to use the Davidson-Weil approach for the evaluation of management while continuing to use the Sandilands approach as in Table 4.7 for the purpose of financial reporting. Whether the additional cost and complexity inherent in using two inventory flow assumptions instead of one could be justified is an empirical question upon which no evidence is currently available.

4.8 Some limitations of this analysis

The fundamental proposal of this chapter has been that a comparison should be made of actual purchasing performance against an *ex post* optimal budget representing those purchases which would have been optimal had the size and timing of the price increase(s) during the budget period been known in advance.[11] This optimal budgeting approach is not new, and its limitations have been well stated in a recent article by Amey [4]. Four of his strictures in particular may prove critical:

(i) It is not possible in optimal budgeting to make interim assessments of performance, prior to the end of the budget period. Clearly, the budget period must have ended for it to be possible to determine what optimal purchases were for that period.

(ii) The ex post optimal budget is optimal only for the period to which it refers. It may be, for example, that a price increase is anticipated at the beginning of the next period, but stocking up in preparation for it would appear simply as an adaptation error in this period's budget. This problem would be particularly acute in the presence of highly uncertain lead times to delivery, since these might well result in stocking up taking place well in advance of the anticipated date of a price increase.

(iii) In real situations, the *ex post* optimum even for a single period may be so tricky to calculate that the effort of so doing cannot be justified. Dealing with inventory problems in isolation, there are EOQ formulae available in the works of Newman [75], Allen and Bunch [2], Machline [65] and Buzacott [21] which deal with most situations in which price increases are anticipated. However, it cannot be denied that for a firm as a whole the *ex post* optimum would be next to impossible to calculate, and further that adherence to the *ex post* optimum for a particular segment of the firm's activities might in some circumstances conflict with optimisation for the firm as a whole.

(iv) Setting as a standard *ex post* optimality will imply that some measure of forecasting and adaptation error must always take place. This omnipresence of error may serve to discourage managerial effort.

The above critique seems to this author to leave the position fairly finely balanced. On the one hand it is clear that the conventional method of measuring purchasing performance through the material price variance is quite likely to give rise to dysfunctional behaviour. Yet while the methods outlined here penalise such behaviour, they have the very substantial drawbacks set out above. Both *ex ante* and *ex post* budget targets may prove inappropriate, the former because of changes during the budget period and the latter because they ignore interrelationships between this and subsequent periods. The best solution, given the present state of the art, may perhaps be of the following nature:

(i) Set budget targets for net realisable cost savings for as far ahead as it is considered worthwhile to predict, and revise them frequently as circumstances change. Use comparisons of actual performance against these *ex ante* targets for short-term control, bearing in mind that an excess of actual over budget net realisable cost savings is not necessarily praiseworthy since it may merely reflect the purchase of greater quantities than are justified by the size of an anticipated price rise. A penalty will have to be paid for this over-buying in terms of higher carrying costs in subsequent periods.

(ii) Compute forecasting and adaptation errors at the end of a budget period, using the forecasting error to detect whether the over-buying mentioned above has taken place. The adaptation error would have to be cautiously interpreted, since adaptation errors can be signalled where what has happened is not poor adaptation but good forecasting for later budget periods.

This use of the *ex post* budget as a check on the *ex ante* budget's analysis rather than as a control tool on its own may perhaps help to avoid the adverse motivational consequences mentioned in point (iv) of Amey's critique above. But there is no denying that this whole area remains in a thoroughly unsatisfactory state. In particular, two developments are urgently required. These are, first, the construction of a better method of measuring adaptation error in a multiperiod context[12], and second, a more explicit consideration of the role of uncertainty. In this chapter, an extremely naive EOQ model was deliberately adopted so as to illustrate basic principles. The analysis would have been considerably more complex if a stochastic model had instead been adopted, incorporating uncertainty as to the demand for the commodity and as to its lead time to delivery. Indeed, the incorporation of stochastic EOQ models within a forecasting/adaptation error framework would seem to constitute an obvious direction for further research.

At this point, though, a cautionary note is in order. There is always a temptation when faced with this sort of problem to search for a global optimum solution without first questioning whether such a search is economically justified. In real life, business is essentially a process of trial-and-error adjustment rather than global optimisation. What really matters, therefore, is whether a proposed control system will motivate managers to achieve results which are sufficiently 'better' than those currently attained to cover the costs of changing from the old system to the new. If building *ex post* targets into an inventory control system will induce purchasing managers to purchase in advance of price increases, then it may be justified even if these targets do not represent optimal states for the firm as a whole.

The theme of trial-and-error adjustment by firms to a changing environment provides a suitable introduction to the last chapter of this book. In it, an attempt will be made in the broadest terms to study the response of firms to a changing inflationary environment, both now and in the future.

5 A Further Outlook

5.1 Inflation and management: Stimulus and response

Though a great deal has been written about the broad social and economic implications of inflation, detailed empirical studies of the process of management under inflationary conditions are not frequently encountered. Indeed, the only currently-available U.K. study of the impact of inflation on management is provided by the management consultants Harbridge House Europe [44]. They used a postal questionnaire to 47 U.K. companies to derive the following results concerning the impact of inflation:

Impact of inflation	% of companies with great impact	% of companies affected
Increasing uncertainty	60	94
Squeezing costs and prices	41	100
Difficulty in planning	37	96
Squeezing liquidity	35	76
Raising cost of finance	26	74
Changes in market place	24	81

These results show the general nature of the stimulus inflation gives to management; their great generality may be inevitable given that inflation has only recently risen to prominence as a generator of major managerial problems in the U.K. A well thought out managerial response to inflation is only likely to be present where inflation has been severe and continued, as in Latin America. Again, it turns out that there are very few analytical studies of management under Latin American conditions (though there is a great deal of descriptive material at the anecdotal level). Probably the most useful study is in the form of a thesis by Saxena [87]. He concentrated upon the Brazilian subsidiaries of U.S. corporations, and compared subsidiaries operating with varying degrees of success in the same industries to see what managerial tactics distinguished the successful subsidiaries from the less successful ones. His conclusion was that if you took a particular industry, the U.S. subsidiaries who operated relatively successfully in it tended to be characterised by their adoption of the following measures, in decreasing order of importance:

  (i) The carrying out of hedging and swap operations.
  (ii) The use of financial leverage.
 (iii) The implementation of periodic price increases.
 (iv) The reduction where possible of operating costs.
  (v) The minimisation of cash-holdings and cash float.
 (vi) The prompt remission of funds to the parent company.

Looking at this list, it is chastening to observe how few of the items on it lie within the scope of this book's coverage. The above items seem to have in common a concern with pricing, with cash management and with operational budgeting generally; there is no doubt that a systematic study of price and cost planning under inflationary conditions is long overdue. This, however, is as far as this book will go in the way of pointing directions for further research. Such directions tend by their very nature to be ill-defined and unhelpful, so that it seems sensible to proceed instead by carrying out three small extensions to the analysis. The first of these will be developed from material presented in Chapter 2, the second from Chapter 3 and the third from Chapter 4. It is hoped that they will act as more substantial guides to future researchers than would a set of perfunctory paragraphs doing no more than indicate the existence of 'Terra Incognita'.

5.2 Three small extensions of the analysis:

(a) Short-term cash budgeting

The Harbridge House study quoted above indicated that accelerating inflation tended to increase managerial uncertainty. It also hinted at the natural reaction – namely to shorten the planning horizon, placing less emphasis on the three-to seven-year long-term plan and more on the annual budget.[1] Where cost-push inflation is associated with falling margins on sales, it is likely to give rise to pressures on liquidity, which are likely in turn to make the annual cash budget into a focus of attention.

Once again, the vehicle for this analysis will be Division Q of Company R, and the task at hand will be to build up a budget for its operating cash flow in 1978. It is possible to place annual cash budgeting within the same framework as capital budgeting was placed in Chapter 2, and to use much of the same terminology.[2] Hence the algebraic symbols employed in this section will largely be the same as those of Chapter 2 – for them reference should be made to the glossary of algebraic symbols at the back of the book. However, some new symbols will have to be introduced, as follows:

Let S_b be the sales revenue from Division Q in 1978, at base prices. It is obtained by multiplying the physical quantities of goods budgeted to be sold in 1978 by prices per unit prevailing at the end of 1977.

Similarly, let L_b, E_b and M_b be the base-cost of labour, expenses and materials respectively for 1978. Their computation involves working out the quantity of labour hours, the volume of expense items and the volume of materials budgeted to be purchased in 1978, then multiplying these physical quantities by end-1977 unit costs.

Assuming that sales take place evenly with a mid-year price increase of $100xp\%$, the budgeted sales revenue for 1978 at current prices may be represented by S_{cb}, where:

$$S_{cb} = (1+0.5xp)S_b \qquad (5-1)$$

With mid-year cost increases and constant volume, labour, expenses and materials for 1978 may be represented by L_{cb}, E_{cb} and M_{cb} respectively, where:

$$L_{cb} = (1+0.5y_Lp)L_b \qquad (5-2)$$

$$E_{cb} = (1+0.5y_ep)E_b \qquad (5-3)$$

$$M_{cb} = (1+0.5y_mp)M_b \qquad (5-4)$$

Now let S_h, M_h and E_h represent actual sales revenues and actual expenditures on materials and expenses in the preceding year of 1977. Then, by reasoning analogous to that of section 2.6 above, Division Q's cash inflow from sales in 1978 C_{sb} is given by:

$$C_{sb} = sS_h+(1-s)S_{cb} \qquad (5-5)$$

Similarly, the cash outflows for expenses and materials (represented by C_{eb} and C_{mb} respectively) may be written as follows:

$$C_{eb} = eE_h+(1-e)E_{cb} \qquad (5-6)$$

$$C_{mb} = mM_h+(1-m)M_{cb} \qquad (5-7)$$

On the assumption that the credit received for labour services is negligible, the cash outflow in respect of labour C_{Lb} is simply given by:

$$C_{Lb} = L_{cb} \qquad (5-8)$$

The object of this exercise has been to derive the budgeted operating cash flow for 1978, represented by C_b. This may now be written compactly as:

$$C_b = C_{sb}-(C_{eb}+C_{mb}+C_{Lb}) \qquad (5-9)$$

It would, of course, be possible to extend this model from its divisional context to provide a complete cash budget for Company R. There is an excellent exposition of corporate cash budget construction in Lawson and Bean [61, chs. 5 and 6], to which the interested reader is referred.

(b) Divisional financial performance in context

The second of these small extensions will take as its starting point the need (expressed in section 3.10) to balance non-financial and financial considerations when assessing the performance of divisional managers. A fear was expressed in section 3.10 that managers assessed exclusively upon a financial measure might neglect those key result areas which did not have immediate implications for that financial measure. Thus a manager assessed exclusively upon his current residual income might neglect the development of new products, on the grounds that the (discretionary) costs of research and development would serve to reduce his residual income now — while hoping to have left the division before the implications for its profitability of his neglect of innovation became apparent.

One approach to this problem would be to treat the financial performance measure as a component in a more wide-ranging index of managerial performance. To give a concrete example, suppose that the performance of Division Q's manager was adjudged to be 1.5 'points' better in 1978 than 1977, this conclusion being derived from the following calculation:

Key result area	Measure	Value in 1977	Value in 1978	Change over year
Personnel	Labour turnover	17.5%	19.1%	− 1.6
Marketing	Share of market	24.1%	26.3%	+ 2.2
Finance	Current residual income as % of budgeted figure	88.3%	91.4%	+ 3.1
Innovation	Proportion of sales revenue from recently-introduced products	67.4%	65.2%	− 2.2
	NET CHANGE (in 'points')			+ 1.5

There is no difficulty in finding ways of criticising the above format. For a start, it quite ignores those areas of managerial responsibility where performance is difficult to quantify, such as the responsibility to develop subordinate managers and the responsibility to manage in a way acceptable to society as a whole. On a more prosaic level, it has been argued in section 3.5 (c) that divisional financial performance cannot be completely represented without considering cash flow as a separate issue from profitability, yet this is not done here. As a last point, the weighting system inherent in the above calculation is arbitrary and may have undesirable side-effects; it may well be easier to get 1 % closer to budgeted residual income than it is to cut labour turnover by 1 %. If this is the case, then a manager wishing to maximise the recorded value of his performance measure will again be driven in the direction of an undue concentration on financial performance. Having said all this, though, the author still feels that this approach possesses considerable potential for development.

(c) *Evaluating purchasing decisions by reference to the
      time value of money*

The analysis of Chapter 4 dealt with a situation in which the objective was to minimise the (undiscounted) sum of ordering, purchasing and carrying costs, after allowing for the value of closing inventory. Relatively little explicit attention was given to the problem of defining a planning horizon, and the time value of money was dealt with only through the medium of carrying costs. This extension focuses more attention upon these considerations; for simplicity it deals with an agricultural product which cannot be purchased all the time, but only at its annual harvest. This product, once bought, cannot be used immediately since it requires a minimum of two years to mature. After two years, the maturation process stops and the product remains unchanged for a further year. However, once it has been stored for three years a rapid process of deterioration sets in, so that it swiftly becomes unusable. The problem facing the purchaser of this product may be illustrated by a time diagram as follows:

t_0 1978 t_1 1979 t_2 1980 t_3

At time t_0 (1st January, 1978) the purchasing manager is asked by production to supply R tons of the product in a mature state at time t_2, and a further R tons at time t_3. His concern is with the most economical way of doing this. A harvest is about to take place at time t_0 (so that the next one will be at time t_1). The product is bought directly from the primary producers; buying is carried out by a small number of firms who do not trade amongst themselves, so that there is no market upon which raw or partially-mature product can be resold.[3] Consequently, the purchasing manager must buy the whole of his requirements for t_2 and t_3 from the t_0 and t_1 harvests.

The range of strategies open to this manager could at their extremes encompass either of strategies A or B below. Both of these strategies will be assumed to be financially feasible, and the analysis will revolve around them. They are as follows:

Strategy A would involve buying R tons of the product at time t_0, and a further R tons at time t_1. The product bought at time t_0 would supply the t_2 requirement, while that bought at t_1 would supply the t_3 requirement.

Strategy B would involve buying $2R$ tons of the product at time t_1, and nothing at time t_1. Then R tons of (two-year-old) product would be available to meet the t_2 requirement, and R tons of (three-year-old) product would be available to meet the t_3 requirement.

The purchasing manager sets out to choose between these strategies, expressing his objective in terms of minimising the terminal value at time t_3 of his purchasing costs. Cash released from inventory is assumed to be reinvested in the real risk-free asset; which (as before) is expected to appreciate at an annual rate of p. The expected carrying cost of the product p.a. is taken as being H, where H is expressed as a percentage of the cost of acquiring the product. (Thus if $H = 0.25$, the implication would be that product which cost £100 to acquire would cost £25 p.a. to store.) Carrying costs are incurred continuously throughout the year, and may therefore be taken as being incurred on average at the mid-year date.

Given his estimates of p and H, the purchasing manager needs to make one further forecast. Before deciding between strategies A and B, he must form some judgement as to the likely values of r_0 and r_1, which represent the replacement costs per ton of raw product at times t_0 and t_1 respectively. Having done this, he can describe the two alternative strategies as involving the following cash outflows at the following times:

Strategy A involves paying out Rr_0 at time t_0, HRr_0 halfway between t_0 and t_1, Rr_1 at time t_1, $H(Rr_0 + Rr_1)$ halfway between t_1 and t_2 and finally HRr_1 halfway between t_2 and t_3.

Strategy B involves paying out $2Rr_0$ at time t_0, $2HRr_0$ halfway between t_0 and t_1 and again halfway between t_1 and t_2, and finally HRr_0 halfway between t_2 and t_3.

Subtracting the outflows under strategy A from those under strategy B yields the *incremental strategy B minus A*. This incremental strategy has associated with it the following cash outflows and inflows (where $t_{0.5}$ represents the point in time halfway between t_0 and t_1, and so on).

	t_0	$t_{0.5}$	t_1	$t_{1.5}$	$t_{2.5}$
Cash outflows	Rr_0	HRr_0		HRr_0	HRr_0
Cash inflows			Rr_1	HRr_1	HRr_1

If the incremental strategy B minus A has a positive net terminal value when compounded at the expected rate of return on the real risk-free

asset p then strategy B clearly has a lower terminal value of purchasing costs than strategy A and is thus to be preferred. The purchasing manager's decision rule consequently becomes:
Implement strategy B if

$$-Rr_0(1+p)^3 - HRr_0(1+p)^{2.5} + Rr_1(1+p)^2 +$$
$$HR(r_1-r_0)(1+p)^{1.5} + HR(r_1-r_0)(1+p)^{0.5} \text{ is positive.}$$

This decision rule may be seen as an integration of the analysis in Chapters 2 and 4, involving as it does both the notions of compounding at the real risk-free rate and of using forecast cost savings (differences in replacement costs) as aids to decision making. In fact, the analysis may be taken a step further, from decision making to decision evaluation. Suppose that strategy B has been implemented, and it is desired to evaluate at time t_1 whether this strategy was appropriate. At time t_1, the actual replacement costs per ton which prevailed at times t_0 and t_1 will be known, and may be denoted by r_{0a} and r_{1a} respectively. Similarly, the actual rate of return on the real risk-free asset for Year 1 (1978) will be known and may be denoted by p_{a1}; the actual carrying cost for Year 1 will also be known, and may be denoted by H_{a1}.

Now if at time t_1 it is found that $r_{1a} \leqslant r_{0a}$, the policy of implementing strategy B must have been incorrect; there have been no cost savings to set against the higher carrying costs of strategy B in Year 1, and to make matters worse the carrying costs of strategy B in Years 2 and 3 must also be greater than or equal to those of strategy A. But what if $r_{1a} > r_{0a}$? This is what might be expected in a period of inflation, and if it proves to be the case then it must make:

$$HR(r_1-r_0)(1+p)^{1.5} > 0 \text{ and } HR(r_1-r_0)(1+p)^{0.5} > 0$$

These are the last two terms in the decision rule given above; since they are positive it must follow that:

$$Rr_1(1+p)^2 > Rr_0(1+p)^3 + HRr_0(1+p)^{2.5}$$

is a sufficient but not a necessary condition for the implementation of strategy B to be endorsed. Dividing through both sides by $R(1+p)^2$, this inequality becomes

$$r_1 > r_0(1+p) + Hr_0\sqrt{1+p}$$

But all the terms in this last inequality relate to Year 1, so that it may more properly be rewritten as:

$$r_{1a} > r_{0a}(1+p_{a1}) + H_{a1}r_{0a}\sqrt{1+p_{a1}}$$

At time t_1, it will be known whether or not this inequality holds; if it does, then this is a sufficient condition for endorsing the implementation of strategy B. In fact, it is only if

$$r_{0a} < r_{1a} \leqslant r_{0a}(1+p_{a1}) + H_{a1}r_{0a}\sqrt{1+p_{a1}}$$

that evaluation of the decision to adopt strategy B has to be postponed to time t_2. So long as r_{1a} lies outside the (rather narrow) range just specified, it will be possible to supply a conclusive evaluation of this purchasing decision only one year after it has been taken. A relatively rapid evaluation of this kind may well help both in assessing the judgement of the purchasing manager and in setting up an error-learning process through which that manager may move toward a gradual improvement in his forecasting ability.

5.3 The permanence of inflationary problems for management

So much, then, for the three extensions. But is it *really* worth following them up? More generally, is it really worth devoting substantial volumes of research resources to the problems posed for management by inflation? The answer to this question must depend upon whether the inflation of the mid-70s is viewed as an isolated phenomenon or as part of an ongoing trend toward a consistently more inflation-prone world economy. This author finds the latter view more plausible, for reasons which will now be explained.

Here, the analysis will lean very heavily upon an excellent article by Panić [76], the Chief Economist at the National Economic Development Office. Writing in mid-1976, he advanced the thesis that rapid inflation is best viewed not as a cause of economic discontinuities but as an outcome of them. These discontinuities arise from the use of coercive power by labour, management and governments; the challenge is to explain why the use of coercive power is becoming more widespread. Panic sees this as being an inevitable by-product of the process of international economic growth, and more specifically of the fact that economic growth starts from different bases and proceeds at different rates as between one country and another.

He starts his analysis by pointing out that rates of inflation have tended, since 1959, to increase from one business cycle to the next throughout the OECD countries, in a way which suggests an underlying causal mechanism independent of once-for-all special factors such as the actions of the OPEC oil cartel. His absolutely critical observation, though, is that it is those countries within the OECD which have relatively low per capita incomes distributed in a relatively unequal way which have sustained the highest rates of inflation. From this, Panić infers the existence of an international 'demonstration effect' whereby improving communications lead people in the 'low income, unequally distributed' countries to become increasingly conscious of the relative inferiority of their living standards. This causes their labour, management and government to unleash collective demands upon local resources which those resources are insufficient to satisfy[4] – and inflation is the inevitable result. What is happening is that aspirations toward the consumption patterns of the richest nations are leading to monetary demands which cannot be filled from local real resources, and hence to a money-goods gap and thus inflation.

In turn, the increasing economic interdependence of nations consequent upon an ever more refined international division of labour causes the inflation of the poorer countries to be transmitted in an attenuated form to the richer ones. The significance of this for an extremely open economy such as the U.K. is obvious, and it must be added that Panić's argument would suggest that as relative living standards in the U.K. continued to fall this would itself cause further inflation to arise domestically. If this scenario is at all plausible then Panić's title, 'The Inevitable Inflation', seems well justified. There can in such circumstances be little argument against the devotion of research resources to the problems of management under inflation; these problems are only too likely to be permanent.

Notes

Chapter 1

1. It seems particularly difficult to defend the validity of divisionalisation where there is substantial serial dependence between divisions, so that a large part of the output of each division is sold to other divisions rather than on the external market. The transfer pricing problem which ensues will not be examined here, but experimental evidence of the problems encountered when managers seek to maximise individual performance criteria in a serially dependent situation is to be found in Baumler [10].

Chapter 2

1. Strictly, such a lender would be sure of protection only against price changes for items included in the Retail Price Index. Even this protection might not be absolute if his purchasing pattern for these items differed from the pattern implicit in the Index weights. More fundamentally, to the extent that the lender's purchases were of items not covered by the Index, he would remain vulnerable to the possibility that these excluded items might rise in price more rapidly than the Index rose. This last point is made by Sarnat [86, p. 842].
2. It should be noted that the tax system of the inflation-prone Israeli economy contains provisions broadly similar to those described in this paragraph. This information is derived from Brenner and Patinkin [18, p. 35].
3. While it is possible by diversification to make the consequences of default on a single advance insignificant, a premium over the default risk-free rate will still be required to compensate for default losses as a whole.
4. In fact, the likelihood that stringent price controls will be imposed probably tends to increase as inflation in consumer prices accelerates, i.e. in precisely those circumstances in which the servicing requirements of debt linked to the Retail Price Index would become particularly onerous.
5. The historical precedent for indexing both interest and principal is provided by France, where this double linking was characteristic of most of the indexed bonds issued prior to 1953. On this, see Rozental [85, p. 522].
6. This computation is based upon equation (2–18).
7. It does not, of course, follow that a specific firm will be able to raise its price for a particular commodity just because the average market price for the range of similar commodities making up the relevant wholesale price index has risen. Herein lies the risk of default, for which indexed interest is a reward.
8. All figures quoted in this chapter are in thousands of pounds sterling, and have been rounded to the nearest thousand. They have to a considerable extent been taken from an actual project.

9. Again, it is Ijiri [51, p. 27] who indicates the existence of this pitfall by stating that:

> 'When managers in a division discuss whether or not they should propose a project to headquarters, arguments are presented both for and against making the proposal. However, once the division decides to make the proposal, everyone suddenly works together to achieve the next objective, gaining approval for the project. Such a united effort decreases the possibility of having the plan vetoed by headquarters and the accompanying embarrassment which rejection would bring to the division.
>
> To assure approval by headquarters, the cash flows of a borderline project tend to be adjusted from realistic estimates to optimistic ones.'

10. This premium was first mentioned in the second paragraph of section 2.1; it is discussed further in section 2.7.

11. It seems, indeed, to have been this fact that stimulated much of the early work on capital investment appraisal in inflation. Fuller [36, p. 266], Bulloch and Duvall [20, p. 570] and Knutson [58, pp. 53–4] all give it prominence, particularly in the context of fixed-price contracts.

12. In an earlier approach to these problems, the author used instead the term 'responsiveness factors' [37, p. 5]. The abandonment of this in favour of 'appreciation factors' reflects the fact that specific cost and price increases cannot strictly be said to represent 'responses' to increases in the Retail Price Index.

13. The index used in this type of comparison may be a published one, as here, or may be generated within the company itself. Arguments in favour of the latter approach are given in Hussey [48, pp. 25–6], and advice on how to implement it is to be found in Voss [97], Berman [13] and Major [66, esp. chs. 5 and 6].

14. It will be appreciated that the date of writing of this text renders the January 1979 index numbers wholly notional.

15. For a further discussion of appreciation factor convergence, the reader is referred to McCosh [69, esp. pp. 37–40].

16. The sum of the cash flows (ΣC_j) in this forecast is 820, which is the same as the sum of the taxable profits from operations (ΣP_j) obtained earlier. This is to be expected, since over the whole life of any venture the total profit is simply the sum of the net cash flows. It will be noted, however, that the cash flows have a different time pattern, reaching their peak later in the project's life than do the profits.

17. Strictly, year j's net change in accrued expenses and prepayments should also be included here, but this is assumed to be negligible.

18. The justification for assuming a constant rate of increase of q throughout the vader project's life is the same as that for assuming a constant rate of increase of p quoted in section 2.5, namely one of simplicity and expedience.

19. While stock appreciation reliefs should also be deducted here, an attempt to do so would run into two major difficulties. The first of these arises from the fact that the current (1976) method of computing reliefs is intended only to be of temporary application, and it is not clear what will replace it. A suggestion by the Inland Revenue for a more permanent method is to be found in the Sandilands Report [83, pp. 360–1], but this represents only a tentative approach.

The second difficulty in computing stock appreciation relief stems from the fact that this relief is currently applicable not only to raw materials, but also to work-in-progress and finished goods stocks. To take into account the latter two types of stock would raise particularly acute forecasting and modelling problems.

20. If a project's acceptance is assumed to affect the amount paid in ACT, the problem then arises of predicting the proportion of its net cash flows which will enter into qualifying distributions. This raises such intractable difficulties that a rule of thumb which (say) reduces the tax lag from twelve to nine months to allow for a 'standard' ACT/MCT mix may well represent the best that can be done.

21. It is not, of course, suggested that Company R would be in the least likely to invest the vader project's proceeds entirely in real risk-free assets. All that matters in this context is that Company R would be *capable* of so doing.

22. The references quoted in Porter, Bey and Lewis [81, p. 639] underline the importance of downside semivariance as a risk measure consistent with managerial thought processes. Managers, it seems, consider risk in terms of the probability of not meeting a financial target. Further support for this view was given by Greer's [42] empirical study of choice among risky investments. The managers he studied made choices which, as Hoskins [46] pointed out, could be convincingly explained by a model using downside semivariance as a risk measure, but which fitted badly within a model using variance instead.

23. Different values for appreciation factors, the rate of increase of the Retail Price Index and so on might be used as between the most likely case and the worst reasonably foreseeable case. The point here is that the circumstances in which each case would arise might well be such as to render different values of these 'headquarters variables' appropriate.

24. See for example Bierman and Smidt [15, chs. 11 and 12].

25. This situation might arise because the outputs of these projects were in an economic sense inferior goods, so people bought more of them (at a constant price) as their incomes fell. Falling incomes would in turn be associated with worsening economic conditions and therefore with declining stock market returns. Consequently the very conditions which caused stock market returns to decline would also cause sales revenues from these projects to rise.

26. It might, for example, be the case that all the projects in the group depended on the same source of raw material supply. If this source were to become unavailable, then clearly all the projects would perform badly together.

27. For a detailed case study of the process by which a capital budget is drawn up as a compromise between the conflicting interests of different participants in a firm, see Carter [23].

Chapter 3

1. It may be worth illustrating this latter case by reference to an extreme example in which an item of product was entirely constructed from components which were obsolete and consequently had their RC>NRV/PV. In computing operating profit, the material cost to be matched against sales revenue would in this example consist of the net

realisable values of each of the components *sold individually* (as distinct from being combined into a final product).

2. For a proposal to deal with the case 5 problem which does not involve straying too far from a Sandilands frame of reference, see Gee and Peasnell [38, pp. 245–247].

3. The costs of research or advertising carried out centrally on a division's behalf would still enter that division's profit statement, being deducted from current residual income in order to arrive at current residual contribution. This latter measure is dealt with in section 3.6.

4. Where, for example, a fixed asset can be resold only for scrap it is likely that its resale value will be quite independent of its replacement cost.

5. Revsine [84, p. 108] calls the situation in which the net cash flows from operating an asset remain constant when its replacement cost increases a Type B increase. He points out that it could arise when an increase in an asset's replacement cost is caused by an increase in the derived demand for that asset's services from another industry. The situation in which the net cash flows from operating an asset actually fall when its replacement cost increases is called by him a Type C increase. An example of such an increase is illustrated in the text.

6. These additional realisable cost savings must be balanced against the higher carrying costs incurred in holding larger inventories. The figure of controllable business profit takes both carrying costs and realisable cost savings into account, while controllable operating profit is struck after deducting carrying costs but before adding in realisable cost savings. Hence it is essential that controllable business profit not controllable operating profit be used to assess the financial performance of the divisional manager. For a fuller exposition of this point, see section 4.4.

7. For an exhaustive justification of this position, see Thomas [92, chs. 3 and 4]. A summary is provided in a later work by him [93, pp. 39–40].

8. In the context of this discussion profit may be taken to mean controllable business profit, but the argument advanced remains valid irrespective of the concept of profit adopted.

9. Strictly, the revenue for 1977 from scrapping the asset would be somewhat greater than the £100 quoted here, since the act of scrapping would take place at the beginning of the year, and the scrap receipts could be reinvested through 1977 to give rise to an end-year figure in excess of £100. However, since this reinvestment would affect the calculations of Division Q's manager and those of Company R's top management to an exactly equal extent, it has been excluded from this exposition.

10. Similarly, if a debt of £10,000 owed by Division Q is paid after three months rather than immediately, Company R will save approximately £375 in overdraft interest and reduce its capital charge to Division Q correspondingly. Again, the appropriate change in the capital charge depends upon the duration and book value of the debt.

11. In reality, this statement could for greater accuracy be drawn up on a monthly or even weekly basis.

12. Depreciation, it should be noted, is not a cost inflicted by the division upon the company. The cost inflicted by a division when it elects to go on holding a fixed asset for a further year is given by:

Interest foregone on its beginning-year NRV + Decline in NRV over year.

If a fixed asset could be sold for £100 at the beginning of a year and £80 at the end, then with an interest rate of 10 % p.a. the (opportunity) cost of retaining that asset over the year would be £100 (1.1)–£80 = £30. A division could justify retaining the asset over the year if by doing so it could amass at least £30 more by the year-end than it could have done without the asset. This £30 magnitude, though, has nothing to do with depreciation, which is no more than the arbitrary allocation over time of a measure (updated or historic) of the outlay required to obtain a stock of fixed asset services.

13. Division Q's management might, however, remain able to exercise some *influence* over debtor and creditor magnitudes by negotiating more or less lengthy periods of credit on its sales and purchases.

14. It is also conceivable that some or all of Division Q's purchasing might be carried out centrally, its orders being combined with those of other divisions to obtain larger quantity discounts. To the extent that this happened, Division Q's manager would be relieved of his responsibility for the capital charge on inventory. The extreme case where purchasing and trade credit administration were both centralised, though, would hardly be consistent with Division Q having separate divisional status at all.

15. This approximation will be exact only if opening and closing fixed asset NRV's for the year are identical.

16. This net realisable value relates to the larger of the following amounts:

(i) that which could be obtained by the sale of Division Q as a going concern

(ii) that which could be obtained by the sale of Division Q's assets, and the discharge of its liabilities, on a piecemeal basis.

It is recognised that both of these amounts can only be estimated with a high degree of subjectivity. The purpose of this exercise, however, is merely to draw attention to the *possibility* that disposing of Division Q might prove profitable; it cannot be in any sense conclusive.

17. A distinction must be made between the short run and the long run here. The net cash flows which would arise from continuing to operate Division Q for a limited period and with minimal new investment must be distinguished from the flows which would arise from the operation of Division Q into the indefinite future with substantial new investment.

18. The usual definition of value added as the difference between sales revenue and all payments made to outside suppliers has been rejected here, on the grounds that its use might distort decisions by divisional management as between buying services from outside and performing them within the division.

A simple example will serve to illustrate this. Suppose that in a budget period a division makes a current residual contribution of £8 on sales of £100, and in doing so incurs costs of £50 for goods and services provided by outside suppliers. This will give the division a ratio of current residual contribution to value added (as broadly defined) of 16 %.

Now suppose that during this budget period the division has spent £9 on a service provided internally which could have been bought from the outside at a cost of £10. Buying the service from outside would have reduced current residual contribution from £8 to £7, but would also have reduced value added from £50 to £40 as the cost of goods and services bought from outside rose from £50 to £60 with unchanged sales of £100. While buying from outside would have been against the company's interest (as reducing current residual contribution) it would have been in the interests of the divisional manager (as improving his current residual contribution to value added ratio from 16% to 17.5%).

This problem may be largely avoided if attention is confined to value added *to materials*. Divisions normally have no option but to buy materials from outside them, so that no decision exists which might be distorted. The only possible exception to this might be where a choice arose between buying a semi-finished product and buying a raw material for processing within the division. The former might then be unduly favoured since it involved adding less value than the latter. But any switch from one to the other would imply the closure (or installation) of raw material processing facilities. This would itself be a capital budgeting decision, and section 3.3 of this chapter has already emphasised that such decisions should not be taken at divisional level.

19. It is true that the existing management can hire additional managers, but they will take time to become familiar with the firm's operations and therefore fully effective. Since this process of familiarisation will involve some 'teaching' by the existing management, there will in any case be a limit to the number of new managers who can be absorbed in any one period.

Chapter 4

1. Carrying costs will not normally vary directly with the purchase price per unit, as they do here. The task of estimating carrying costs in practice has recently been the subject of a detailed study by Lambert [59].

2. For a slightly more elaborate EOQ model in which a cost increase is forecast to take place at a time when there will still be some stock in hand, and under circumstances in which there is a significant lead time to delivery, see Machline [65, pp. 61–4].

3. The higher carrying costs of situation (iv) will, of course, persist into 1979. By the end of 1979, however, the effects of the large purchase in 1977 will have substantially worked themselves out. Comparing the total costs of the policies in situations (iii) and (iv) over the whole of 1977–79 it is found that situation (iii) involves a total cost of £84,331 while situation (iv) involves a total cost of £82,007. But situation (iii) leaves 236 units in stock at the end of 1979 while situation (iv) leaves only 150 units. Valuing this 86-unit difference at the replacement cost of £28 per unit gives a total value of £2408, to be compared with the incremental cost of situation (iii) over situation (iv), which is only £2324. Thus the (optimal) situation (iii) is seen to have a lower value of ordering, purchasing and carrying costs per unit than has situation (iv).

4. It should be noted here that controllable ordering costs frequently turn out to be negative, since there is a saving where fewer orders are made during a year in one of situations (ii), (iii) or (iv) than would have been made during that year in situation (i).

5. It is assumed throughout this chapter that the funds available to Division Q are sufficient to finance any size of purchase. If this is not the case, then part of the forecasting error may reflect the cost savings foregone where cash shortage dictates the purchase of a suboptimally small quantity (i.e. less than Q_o units) immediately prior to the price increase. Another possibility is that part of the adaptation error (q.v.) may be attributable to the purchase, as a result of cash shortage, of suboptimally small order quantities (i.e. less than Q_{2a} units) subsequent to the price increase.

   To the extent that forecasting and adaptation errors arise as a result of cash shortages, they may be deemed to lie outside the control of the purchasing manager.

6. In situation (iv), it was forecast that the cost per unit of the commodity would rise to £29, while in situation (ii) the forecast was for a rise to £26. The actual increase was to £28, so that situation (ii) involved an error of £2 in a downward direction while situation (iv) involved a smaller error of £1 in an upward direction. Yet Table 4.4 shows a 50.5% forecasting error in situation (iv) and only a 18.2% error in situation (ii).

7. The ensuing argument depends upon the material price variance being taken at the date of purchase rather than when the commodity is used (resold). This procedure has been widely advocated as a device for producing timely cost variance analyses, notably in Horngren [45, p. 196].

8. This point was originally made by Gordon [39, pp. 8–9]. As long ago as 1963, he proposed a control system which when applied to the purchases in situations (i) and (v) yields for 1977 a favourable 'purchasing department variance' of £304 in each situation, thus leaving the purchasing manager indifferent as between situations (i) and (v). In producing this result, Gordon's system fails to satisfy the need from a corporate point of view to instil a positive preference for situation (i). It is also true that Gordon's system is incapable of distinguishing between forecasting and adaptation errors.

9. It is only in 1977 that the end-of-year unit cost for the commodity differs from its average unit cost for the year. Consequently, 1977 is the only year in which the Davidson-Weil formulae will produce a split between operating profit and cost savings which differs from that obtained by applying the Sandilands approach.

10. On the other hand, it may be argued that since under Sandilands [83, paras. 607–11] depreciation is computed by reference to the *end-of-year* value of fixed assets, application of the Davidson-Weil formulae would have the beneficial effect of rendering the treatment of inventory consistent with that of fixed assets.

11. A summary statistic derived from this comparison which might be used for the assessment of purchasing managers relative to one another is:

$$\frac{\text{forecasting error} + \text{adaptation error}}{\text{optimal controllable net cost savings}} \times 100\%$$

   On the face of it, the lower the value of this statistic the better is the manager's performance–though regard must be had to the asymmetry of the forecasting error about the optimal situation (q.v.).

12. A start could be made on this problem if purchasing managers were required

to state at the end of each budget period whether and to what extent the closing stock had been built up over the minimum required for day-to-day operations in anticipation of subsequent purchase price increases. Any such 'speculative stocks' would then be removed from the calculation of this period's adaptation error, but would enter into the calculation of forecasting error for the next period.

Chapter 5

1. Empirical evidence on this point is scanty, but Killpack [56, pp. 11–12] documents the withdrawal in the face of inflation of a formal five-year planning process and its replacement with a simpler and more impressionistic system.
2. Where terminology identical to that of Chapter 2 is used here, the implicit assumption is that values appropriate for the vader project are also appropriate for Division Q as a whole. For example, the unqualified use of the symbol x both here and in Chapter 2 implies that the same appreciation factor for the unit price of output relative to the Retail Price Index is appropriate both for the vader project's output and for the aggregate output of Division Q.
3. In fact, an attempt by a buying firm to resell some of its product to one of the competitors who buy against it would probably be interpreted as evidence of financial instability on the selling firm's part. Once news of such an attempt became known to the industry as a whole, it might well damage the selling firm's ability to raise credit.

   (The whole of this extension is based upon a real industrial situation, which cannot be identified for reasons of confidentiality.)
4. In this context, he points out that the higher the level of *per capita* income in a country, the lower in general is the number of days lost in strikes. The suggested explanation is that strike activity is at least in part an outcome of feelings of relative deprivation on an international scale.

Glossary of Algebraic Symbols Used

A : the cost of placing an order.

b : rate of Regional Development Grant.

B_j : tax-deductible premium on redemption of indexed debt in year j.

c_a : realisable cost saving on inventory actually achieved.

c_m : that portion of the realisable cost saving on inventory which may be attributed to the purchasing manager's skill.

c_n : realisable cost saving on inventory associated with an inventory policy which is wholly passive toward forecast price changes.

c_o : realisable cost saving on inventory associated with the optimal inventory policy.

C : the cost of purchasing a unit of inventory.

C_b : Division Q's operating cash flow for the budget year (1978).

C_{eb} : Division Q's cash outflow for expenses in the budget year (1978).

C_{ej} : cash outflow for expenses in year j.

C_j : operating cash flow in year j.

C_{kj} : year j's cash outflow in payment for capital expenditures.

C_{Lb} : Division Q's cash outflow for labour in the budget year (1978).

C_{Lj} : cash outflow for labour in year j.

C_{mb} : Division Q's cash outflow for materials in the budget year (1978).

C_{mj} : cash outflow for materials in year j.

C_{sb} : Division Q's cash inflow from sales in the budget year (1978).

C_{sj} : year j's cash inflow from sales.

d : the lag between acquiring an item of material and its being charged out to production.

D : the annual demand in units for a commodity held in inventory.

D_j : amount of capital allowances to be deducted in arriving at taxable profits of year j.

e : lag in payment for expenses.

E_b : base-cost of expenses for Division Q in 1978.

E_{cb} : current cost of expenses for Division Q in 1978.

E_{cj} : current cost of expenses incurred in year j.

E_h : expenses for Division Q in year prior to budget (1977).

E_j : base-cost of expenses incurred in year j.

F_j : interest payable on indexed debt in year j.

g : year of raising of indexed debt repaid in year j.

G_{cj} : year j's cash inflow from Regional Development Grants.

h : $= j - 0.5$.

H : expected carrying cost of inventory, expressed as a percentage p.a. of its unit cost C.

H_{aj} : actual carrying cost of inventory during year j, expressed as a percentage p.a. of its unit cost C.

H_j : net realisable value (at base-prices) of plant and machinery at end of year j.

i : rate of interest p.a. payable on indexed debt.

J_{aj} : average cost per unit of inventory prevailing during year j.

J_{bj} : cost per unit of opening inventory prevailing at the beginning of year j.

J_{cj} : cost per unit of closing inventory prevailing at the end of year j.

k : lag in payment for capital expenditures.

K_{cj} : capital expenditure incurred in year j at current prices.

K_j : capital expenditure incurred in year j at base prices.

L_b : base-cost of labour for Division Q in 1978.

L_{cb} : current cost of labour for Division Q in 1978.

L_{cj} : current cost of labour in year j.

L_j : base-cost of labour in year j.

m : lag in payment for materials.

M_b : base-cost of materials for Division Q in 1978.

M_{bj} : base-cost of materials bought in year j.

M_{cb} : current cost of materials for Division Q in 1978.

M_{cj} : current cost of materials bought in year j.

M_h : cost of materials for Division Q in year prior to budget (1977).

M_{hj} : cost of materials used (on FIFO basis) in year j.

M_{uj} : base-cost of materials used in year j.

n : number of years to horizon date for project assessment.

p : expected rate of change p.a. in the Retail Price Index.

p_{aj} : actual rate of change experienced in the Retail Price Index during year j.

P_a : actual cost increase for commodity held in inventory.

P_e : expected cost increase for commodity held in inventory.

P_f : forecast cost increase for commodity held in inventory associated specifically with situation (iv) in section 4.4.

P_j : year j's taxable profit from operations.

q : forecast rate of change p.a. of the wholesale price index relating to the outputs of the mechanical engineering industry.

Q : the optimal order quantity to be purchased, given particular circumstances represented by suffixes.

Q_j : scrap receipts at current prices in year j.

r_j : replacement cost of a ton of raw agricultural product at time t_j.

R_{fj} : materials inventory at FIFO cost, beginning of year j.

R_{gj} : materials inventory at FIFO cost, end of year j.

R_j : stock of materials (at base-cost) to be held at beginning of year j.

s : lag in payment for sales.

S_b : sales revenue for Division Q as a whole (at base prices) in 1978.

S_{cb} : sales revenue for Division Q as a whole (at current prices) in 1978.

S_{cj} : sales revenue for year j at current prices.

S_h : sales revenue for Division Q in year prior to budget (1977).

S_j : sales revenue for year j at base prices.

t : forecasted rate of Corporation Tax.

T_{cj} : cash flow in year j associated with Corporation Tax.

T_j : taxable profit for year j.

w : appreciation factor for unit capital costs relative to the Retail Price Index.

W_j : change in invested working capital over year j.

x : appreciation factor for unit prices of output relative to the Retail Price Index.

X_j : cash outflow for debt repayment in year j.

y_e : appreciation factor for unit cost of expenses relative to the Retail Price Index.

y_L : appreciation factor for unit cost of labour relative to the Retail Price Index.

y_m : appreciation factor for unit cost of materials relative to the Retail Price Index.

z : appreciation factor for scrap receipts relative to the Retail Price Index.

Bibliography

1. Adelson, R. M., 'Discounted Cash Flow–Can we Discount it? A Critical Examination', *Journal of Business Finance*, vol. 2, no. 2, (Summer 1970) 50–66.
2. Allen, G. and Bunch, R. G., 'Be Sure it Pays to Stock Up', *Purchasing*, (18 Nov 1965) 85–9.
3. American Accounting Association, *A Statement of Basic Accounting Theory* (Evanston, Illinois, 1966).
4. Amey, L. R., 'Hindsight v. Expectations in Performance Measurement', in Amey, L. R. (ed.), *Readings in Management Decision* (Longman, 1973) pp. 258–72.
5. Amey, L. R., 'Tomkins on Residual Income', *Journal of Business Finance and Accounting*, vol. 2, no. 1 (Spring 1975) 55–68.
6. Amey, L. R. and Egginton, D. A., *Management Accounting: A Conceptual Approach* (Longman, 1973).
7. Anthony, R. N., 'Management Accounting for the Future', *Sloan Management Review* (Spring 1972) 17–34.
8. Anthony, R. N., *Accounting for the Cost of Interest* (Lexington Books, 1975).
9. Ashton, R. and Morrell, J., *Inflation and Business Management* (Economic Forecasters Publications Ltd, 1975).
10. Baumler, J. V., 'Defined Criteria of Performance in Organizational Control', *Administrative Science Quarterly*, vol. 16, no. 3, (Sep 1971) 340–9.
11. Baxter, W. T., *Accounting Values and Inflation* (McGraw-Hill, 1975).
12. Bell, P. W., 'Optimizing Inventory Acquisition and Holding Policy in the Face of Price Changes', in *Collected Papers of the American Accounting Association's Annual Meeting, August 18–20, 1975*, (American Accounting Association, 1976) 435–51.
13. Berman, G. R., 'Constructing and Using a Company Cost Index', *The Business Quarterly*, vol. 41, no. 2 (Summer 1976) 50–3.
14. Bhatia, K. B., 'Index-Linking of Financial Contracts: A Survey of the State-of-the-Arts', (Research Report 7412, Department of Econmics, University of Western Ontario, 1974).
15. Bierman, H. and Smidt, S., *The Capital Budgeting Decision*, (4th ed.) (Collier Macmillan, 1975).
16. Bradford, W. D., *Inflation, the Value of the Firm and the Cost of Capital* (unpublished Ph.D. thesis, Ohio State University, 1971).
17. Branford, Susan, 'Brazilian Industry II: Providing the Finance', *Financial Times* (27 May 1975) 35.
18. Brenner, R. and Patinkin, D., 'Indexation in Israel', (Research Report no.76, Department of Economics, The Hebrew University of Jerusalem, 1975).

19. Brown, C. C., 'Inflation-Costs and Prices: The Importance of Cash Flow', *The Accountant* (22 Apr 1976) 473–5.

20. Bulloch, J. and Duvall, R. M., 'Adjusting Rate of Return and Present Value for Price Level Changes', *Accounting Review*, vol. XL, no. 3, (July 1965) 569–73.

21. Buzacott, J. A., 'Economic Order Quantities with Inflation', *Operational Research Quarterly*, vol. 26, no. 3 (Aug 1975) 553–8.

22. Carsberg, B. and Hope, A., *Business Investment Decisions under Inflation* (The Institute of Chartered Accountants in England and Wales, 1976).

23. Carter, E. E., 'The Behavioral Theory of the Firm and Top-Level Corporate Decisions', *Administrative Science Quarterly*, vol. 16, no. 4 (Dec 1971) 413–28.

24. Carter, R. and Voss, C., 'Inflation and Investment', *Management Today* (Nov 1972) 58, 61, 64, 68.

25. Chambers, R. J., *Current Cost Accounting–A Critique of the Sandilands Report* (Occasional Paper no. 11, International Centre for Research in Accounting, University of Lancaster, 1976).

26. Cornell, W. B., *Essays on the Relationship between Interest Rates and Inflationary Expectations* (unpublished Ph.D. thesis, Stanford University, 1975).

27. Cox, B. and Hewgill, J. C. R., *Management Accounting in Inflationary Conditions* (The Institute of Cost and Management Accountants, 1976).

28. Dale, R., 'OECD Forecasts 8% Inflation Rate for Rest of Decade', *Financial Times* (11 June 1976) 1.

29. Davidson, S. and Weil, R. L., 'On Holding Gains and Losses and the Evaluation of Management', *Accounting Review* (July 1974) 524–7.

30. DeVoe, R. F., 'Brazil's Experience with Indexing', *Financial Analysts Journal,* vol. 30, no. 5 (Sep–Oct 1974) 32–41, 87.

31. Drucker, P. F., *The Practice of Management* (Harper and Brothers, 1954).

32. Edwards, E. O. and Bell, P. W., *The Theory and Measurement of Business Income* (University of California Press, 1961).

33. Edwards, J. B., 'Adjusted DCF Rate of Return', *Management Accounting (N.A.A.)* (Jan 1973) 45–9.

34. Fisher, I., *The Theory of Interest* (New York: Macmillan, 1930).

35. Franko, L. G., 'The Move toward a Multidivisional Structure in European Organizations', *Administrative Science Quarterly*, vol. 19, no. 4 (Dec 1974) 493–506.

36. Fuller, I. D., 'Capital Investment Decisions–How to Provide for Inflation', *The Australian Accountant* (May 1967) 259–70.

37. Gee, K. P., 'Capital Project Appraisal in Inflation: A Survey', (paper presented to the Sep 1974 meeting of the British Accounting and Finance Association held at Manchester Business School).

38. Gee, K. P, and Peasnell, K. V., 'A Pragmatic Defence of Replacement Cost', *Accounting and Business Research*, no. 24 (Autumn 1976) 242–9.

39. Gordon, M., 'Toward a Theory of Responsibility Accounting Systems', *N.A.A. Bulletin* (Dec 1963) 3–9.

40. Gordon, M. J. and Halpern, P. J., 'Cost of Capital for a Division of a

Firm', *Journal of Finance* (Sep 1974) 1153–63.

41. Greenwood, R. G., *Managerial Decentralization* (Lexington Books, 1974).

42. Greer, W. R., 'Theory versus Practice in Risk Analysis: An Empirical Study', *Accounting Review*, vol XLIX, no. 3 (July 1974) 496–505.

43. Greer, W. R., 'Inflation and Asset Performance Measurement', *Management Accounting (N.A.A.)* (Jan 1976) 49–52.

44. Harbridge House Europe, 'Management's Reaction to Inflation', *European Business*, no. 44 (Spring 1975) 3–5.

45. Horngren, C. T., *Cost Accounting: A Managerial Emphasis*, (3rd edition) (Prentice-Hall, 1972).

46. Hoskins, C. G., 'Theory versus Practice in Risk Analysis: An Empirical Study: A Comment', *Accounting Review*, vol. L, no. 4 (Oct 1975) 835–8.

47. Hussey, D. E., 'Strategic Planning and Inflation', *Long Range Planning*, vol 9, no. 2 (Apr 1976) 24–30.

48. Hussey, D. E., *Inflation and Business Policy* (Longman, 1976).

49. Huyck, P. M., 'Brazil Vitalizes its Capital Market', *Columbia Journal of World Business*, vol. 7 (Nov–Dec 1972) 58–66.

50. Ibbotson, R. G. and Sinquefield, R. A., 'Stocks, Bonds, Bills and Inflation: Simulations of the Future (1976–2000)', *Journal of Business*, vol. 49, no. 3 (July, 1976) 313–38.

51. Ijiri, Y., *Theory of Accounting Measurement* (Studies in Accounting Research, no. 10, American Accounting Association, 1975).

52. Inflation Accounting Steering Group, *Guidance Manual on Current Cost Accounting* (Tolley and the ICAEW, 1976).

53. Jones, D. A., 'Capital Budgeting: Mixing Up the Balance Sheet', *Financial Executive* (Apr 1976) 45–8.

54. Kafka, A., 'Indexing for Inflation in Brazil', in Giersch, H. et al., *Essays on Inflation and Indexation* (American Enterprise Institute for Public Policy Research, Domestic Affairs Study 24, 1974) pp. 87–98.

55. Keane, S. M., 'The Cost of Capital and the Relevance of Non-diversifiable Risk', *Journal of Business Finance and Accounting*, vol. 1, no. 1 (Spring 1974) 129–44.

56. Killpack, J. R., 'Planning in an Inflationary Environment', *Managerial Planning* (Jan–Feb 1976) 10–13.

57. King, P., 'Is the Emphasis of Capital Budgeting Theory Misplaced?', *Journal of Business Finance and Accounting*, vol. 2, no. 1 (Spring 1975) 69–82.

58. Knutson, P., *The Effect and Treatment of Price Level Changes in the Investment Decisions of Industrial Firms* (unpublished Ph.D. thesis, University of Michigan, 1965).

59. Lambert, D. M., *The Development of an Inventory Costing Methodology: A Study of the Costs Associated with Holding Inventory* (unpublished Ph.D. thesis, The Ohio State University, 1975).

60. Lawson, G. H., 'The Rationale for Measuring the Cost of Working Capital', (paper presented to a conference on 'Working Capital Management in Advanced Technological Societies', University of Illinois at Urbana-Champaign, Apr 1975).

61. Lawson, G. H. and Bean, D. G., *Enterprise Valuation: A Cash Flow*

Approach (Union Européene des Experts Comptables Economiques et Financiers, forthcoming).

62. Lawson, G. H. and Stark, A. W., 'The Concept of Profit for Fund Raising', (paper presented to a meeting of the Royal Economic Society, University of Sussex, Sep 1975).

63. The Lex Column, 'Novel Funding by British Steel', *Financial Times* (12 Nov 1975) 42.

64. Logue, D. E. and Willett, T. D., 'A Note on the Relation between the Rate and Variability of Inflation', *Economica*, vol. 43, no. 170, (May 1976) 151–8.

65. Machline, C., *Price Level Changes and the Inventory Policy of the Firm* (unpublished Ph.D. thesis, Stanford University, 1971).

66. Major, R. D., *A Corporate Cost-of-Living Index* (unpublished Ph.D. thesis, University of Pittsburgh, 1973).

67. Management Control Project, 'Preliminary Results from a Research Project on Management Control in Large Enterprises', (unpublished working paper, Manchester Business School, 1972).

68. Marris, R., *The Economic Theory of 'Managerial' Capitalism* (Macmillan, 1964).

69. McCosh, A. M., 'Inflationary Adjustment of Some Elements of the Planning and Control Cycle in Investment Centres', *Management International Review*, vol. 16, no. 4 (1976) 35–49.

70. McMahon, T. J., 'Brázil: A Maturing Capital Market Seeks Accelerated Improvements in Accountancy', *International Journal of Accounting Education and Research*, vol. 8, no. 1 (Fall 1972) 77–87.

71. Merrett, A. J. and Sykes, A., *The Finance and Analysis of Capital Projects*, (2nd ed.) (Longman, 1973).

72. Morgan, J. and Luck, M., *Managing Capital Investment* (Rugby: Mantec Publications, 1973).

73. Morley, M. F., *The Fiscal Implications of Inflation Accounting* (London: The Institute for Fiscal Studies and the Institute of Chartered Accountants in England and Wales, 1974).

74. Naddor, E., *Inventory Systems* (John Wiley, 1966).

75. Newman, R. G., 'Analysis of Forward Buying', *Production and Inventory Management* (Apr 1967) 64–70.

76. Panić, M., 'The Inevitable Inflation', *Lloyds Bank Review*, no. 121 (July 1976) 1–15.

77. Penrose, Edith T., *The Theory of the Growth of the Firm* (Basil Blackwell, 1959).

78. Petri, E., 'Holding Gains and Losses as Cost Savings: A Comment on Supplementary Statement No. 2 on Inventory Valuation', *Accounting Review* (July 1973) 483–8.

79. Petri. E. and Minch, R., 'Evaluation of Resource Acquisition Decisions by the Partitioning of Holding Activity'. *Accounting Review* (July 1974) 455–64.

80. Petry, G. H., *A Comparison of Incremental Financing with Book and Market Value Proportions for Estimating Weighted Average Cost of Capital and an Analysis of the Use of Capital Budgeting Techniques by Large Corporations* (unpublished D.B.A. thesis, University of Col-

orado, 1974).

81.   Porter, R. B., Bey, R. P. and Lewis D. C., 'The Development of a Mean-Semivariance Approach to Capital Budgeting', *Journal of Financial and Quantitative Analysis*, vol. 10, no. 4 (Nov 1975) 639–51.

82.   Reilly, R. R. and Wecker, W. E., 'On the Weighted Average Cost of Capital: Reply', *Journal of Financial and Quantitative Analysis*, vol 10, no. 2 (June 1975) 367.

83.   *Report of the Inflation Accounting Committee* (HMSO, Cmnd. 6225, Sep 1975).

84.   Revsine, L., *Replacement Cost Accounting* (Prentice-Hall, 1973).

85.   Rozental, A. A., 'Variable Return Bonds–The French Experience', *Journal of Finance* (Dec 1959) 520–30.

86.   Sarnat, M., 'Purchasing Power Risk, Portfolio Analysis and the Case for Index-Linked Bonds', *Journal of Money, Credit and Banking* (Aug 1973) 836–45.

87.   Saxena, N. D., *Effectiveness of Measures Taken by U. S. Corporations to Protect their Investments and Profitability in the Face of Hyperinflation in Brazil during 1960–1970* (unpublished D.B.A. thesis, Kent State University, 1973).

88.   Shank, J. K., *Price Level Adjusted Statements and Management Decisions* (New York: Financial Executives Research Foundation, 1975).

89.   Shohet, P. S. D. and Westwick, C. A., *Investment Appraisal and Inflation*, Research Committee Occasional Paper no. 7 (The Institute Of Chartered Accountants in England and Wales, 1976).

90.   Solomons, D., *Divisional Performance: Measurement and Control* (Irwin, 1965).

91.   Taylor, Nelson Investment Services, 'The Why and the How of Company Investment', *The Director* (Nov 1970) 334–9.

92.   Thomas, A. L., *The Allocation Problem in Financial Accounting Theory*, (Studies in Accounting Research no. 3, American Accounting Association, 1969).

93.   Thomas, A. L., *The Allocation Problem: Part Two*, (Studies in Accounting Research no. 9, American Accounting Association, 1974).

94.   Tomkins, C., *Financial Planning in Divisionalised Companies* (Accountancy Age Books, 1973).

95.   Tomkins, C., 'Residual Income–A Rebuttal of Professor Amey's Arguments', *Journal of Business Finance and Accounting*, vol. 2, no. 2 (Summer 1975) 161–8.

96.   Tweedie, D. P., 'Management's Changing Attitudes towards Inflation 1968–75', *Industrial Relations Journal*, vol. 7, no. 1 (Spring 1976) 4–14.

97.   Voss, C., 'Development of Specific Indices for Measuring Inflation', *The Business Quarterly*, vol. 40, no. 4 (Winter 1975) 51–6.

98.   West, C. J. (ed.), *Inflation: A Management Guide to Company Survival* (Associated Business Programmes, 1976).

99.   Wiles, P., 'Cost Inflation and the State of Economic Theory', *Economic Journal*, vol. 83, no. 330 (June 1973) 377–98.

100. Williamson, O. E., *Corporate Control and Business Behavior* (Prentice-Hall, 1970).

Author Index

Adelson, R. M., 31
Allen, G., 91
American Accounting Association, 2
Amey, L. R., 49, 70, 91
Anthony, R. N., 49
Ashton, R., 9

Baumler, J. V., 103
Baxter, W. T., 40
Bean, D. G., 97
Bell, P. W., 57, 70
Berman, G. R., 104
Bey, R. P., 32, 105
Bhatia, K. B., 9
Bierman, H., 105
Bradford, W. D., 49
Branford, Susan, 8
Brenner, R., 103
Brown, C. C., 21
Bulloch, J., 104
Bunch, R. G., 91
Buzacott, J. A., 91

Carsberg, B., 35
Carter, E. E., 105
Carter, R., 19
Chambers, R. J., vii
Cornell, W. B., 7
Cox, B., 4

Dale, R., 1
Davidson, S., 90
DeVoe, R. F., 9
Drucker, P. F., 65
Duvall, R. M., 104

Edwards, E. O., 57
Edwards, J. B., 17
Egginton, D. A., 70

Fisher, I., 32
Franko, L. G., 3
Fuller, I. D., 104

Gee, K. P., viii, 106

Gordon, M., 109
Gordon, M. J., 50
Greenwood, R. G., 66
Greer, W. R., 19, 105

Halpern, P. J., 50
Harbridge House Europe, 94
Hewgill, J. C. R., 4
Hope, A., 35
Horngren, C. T., 109
Hoskins, C. G., 105
Hussey, D. E., 4, 104
Huyck, P. M., 8

Ibbotson, R. G., 1
Ijiri, Y., 15, 104
Inflation Accounting Steering Group, vii, 77, 88

Jones, D. A., 11

Kafka, A., 6, 9
Keane, S. M., 7
Killpack, J. R., 110
King, P., 43
Knutson, P., 17, 19, 104

Lambert, D. M., 108
Lawson, G. H., 24, 97
Lewis, D. C., 32, 105
'Lex', 11
Logue, D. E., 16
Luck, M., 43

McCosh, A. M., 104
McMahon, T. J., 9, 10
Machline, C., 91, 108
Major, R. D., 104
Management Control Project, Manchester Business School, 43
Marris, R., 63
Merrett, A. J., 29
Minch, R., 70
Morgan, J., 43
Morley, M. F., vii

Index

Morrell, J., 4

Naddor, E., 72
Newman, R. G., 91

Panić, M., 101
Patinkin, D., 103
Peasnell, K. V. viii, 106
Penrose, Edith T., 62
Petri, E., 70, 90
Petry, G. H., 50
Porter, R. B., 32, 105

Reilly, R. R., 50
Revsine, L., 106
Rozental, A. A., 103

Sandilands Report, vii, 37, 40, 73, 88, 104, 109
Sarnat, M., 103
Saxena, N. D., 94
Shank, J. K., vii

Shohet, P. S. D., 16
Sinquefield, R. A., 1
Smidt, S., 105
Solomons, D., 43, 49, 52
Stark, A. W., 24
Sykes, A., 29

Taylor, Nelson Investment Services, 43
Thomas, A. L., 106
Tomkins, C., 42, 49, 60
Tweedie, D. P., 4

Voss, C., 19, 104

Wecker, W. E., 50
Weil, R. L., 90
West, C. J., 4
Westwick, C. A., 16
Wiles, P., 19
Willett, T. D., 16
Williamson, O. E., 3, 35, 43

Subject Index

Adaptation:
  error, 83–8, 92, 109
  optimal, 79
Appreciation factors, 17–19, 21, 23, 104, 110

Banks:
  lending against fixed assets, 11, 54
  overdraft lending, 37–9, 48–52, 55–6
  response to real risk-free asset, 7, 10
Budgeting:
  capital, 12–35
  cash, 55–6, 95–7
  optimal, 76–7, 91–2

Capital:
  allowances, 26
  asset pricing model, 34
  charge, 38, 48–62
  controllable in division, 42–4, 52–3, 107
  costs for project, 21, 23
  rationing, 5
  return on, 38, 67–9
  weighted average cost of, 5, 11, 49–50
Capital projects:
  bias in submission, 43–4, 56–8, 67–9, 104
  horizon date, 29
  planning, 6–35
  portfolio considerations, 33–5
  postauditing, 5
Carrying costs, 71, 98–9, 106, 108
Cash flow:
  components of NTV, 30
  lag behind accruals, 22–3, 55–6, 96
  operating, 22, 95–7, 104, 107
  to individual fixed assets, 48, 106
  to the equity, 29, 36
Corporation Tax, 26–7, 105
Cost of sales adjustment, 88–91
Cost savings:
  controllable, 78
  controllable net, 79–84, 86–91, 109
  net realisable, 75–7, 84, 92
  optimal, 76, 86

realisable on inventory, 74, 100–1, 106

Debt:
  fixed interest, 7–8, 37
  long-term indexed, 8–9
  short-term indexed, 9–11, 24–6, 29, 103
Disposal investigations, 61–2
Division:
  avoidable cost, 59
  cost of capital, 50
  defined, 3
  performance measure, 37, 58–60, 65–6, 97–8
Divisionalisation:
  advantages, 35, 43
  limitations, 103
  pervasiveness, 3

Equity:
  cash flows to the, 29, 36
  use of, 10–11
Expansion investigations, 62–3

Fixed assets:
  capital charge on, 52–4
  depreciation, 42–3, 68, 106–7, 109
  financing, 11
Forecasting:
  error, 81–8, 92, 109
  of appreciation factors, 17–19, 104
  of inflation, 1, 16

Historic cost:
  in divisional performance measurement, 54–5
  price level adjusted, vii–viii
Holding gains:
  realisable on fixed assets, 44–5, 48
  realisable on inventory, 46–8, 70–93

Inflation:
  forecasts, 1, 16
  inevitability of, 101–2
  managerial responses, 94–5

Interest:
  as a divisional cost, 48–52, 106
  on indexed debt, 25–6
Inventory:
  at historic cost, 54–5
  at value to the business, 41
  economic order quantity, 70–2, 91–2, 108
  in capital budgeting, 13–14, 20, 104–5
  Sandilands flow assumption, 88–91

Key result areas, 65–6, 97–8

Management:
  and shareholder interests, 34–5, 105
  as constraint on growth, 62–3, 108
  assessment of divisional, 58–9, 64–6, 74
  control over capital spending, 14–15, 43, 46–7
  discretion of divisional, 38–9, 59–60
  use of price-level adjusted statements, vii
  views on inflation, 4, 94
Material price variance, 83, 85–6, 92, 109

Net realisable value:
  fixed assets, 54, 61–2, 106–7
  inventory, 41, 54, 105–6
  of a division, 107
Net terminal value, 28–33, 98–101

Opportunity cost:
  of assets, 53–5
  of division, 59, 61–2

Planning and control cycle, 2
Present value, 28, 40–1
Price control, 9, 103
Price—base and current, 12
Profit:
  and net cash flow, 3–4, 22–3, 55–6
  divisional statement, 39
  on a product, 63
  taxable, 26
  taxable from operations, 20–1, 104
Purchasing, 39, 46–7, 70–93, 98–101
Purchasing manager:
  assessment, 74–5, 82–3, 92, 100–1, 109–10

behaviour, 71–3, 76–7, 82–6, 90–1

Ratio maximisation, 64–5
Real risk-free asset:
  as reinvestment medium, 28, 29, 99–100, 105
  described, 6–7, 103
Regional Development Grants, 27–8
Replacement cost:
  minimisation problem, 98–101
  or market rule, 40–1, 74
Residual:
  contribution, 58–63, 106
  income, 38–58
Responsibility accounting, 42
Risk:
  analysis, 29, 31
  as downside semivariance, 32–3, 105
  aversion, 32
  of ruin, 33

Sales manager assessment, 74
Scrapping:
  decisions and capital charges, 52–4
  receipts from, 23, 106
Sensitivity analysis, 31
Staff at divisional headquarters, 14–15, 35–6
Stock appreciation relief, 104–5

Tax:
  adjusted for inflation, vii–viii
  payable, 26–7
  treatment of real risk-free assets, 6, 25–6, 103

Value:
  added to materials, 62–3, 107–8
  book, for debtors and creditors, 55–6, 106
  concepts of, vii
  to the business, 40–1

Wholesale price index, 10, 24, 104
Working capital:
  indexed debt-financed, 11–12, 24
  required over time, 24